CURRICULUM AS
MEDITATIVE INQUIRY

Curriculum Studies Worldwide

This series supports the internationalization of curriculum studies worldwide. At this historical moment, curriculum inquiry occurs within national borders. Like the founders of the International Association for the Advancement of Curriculum Studies, we do not envision a worldwide field of curriculum studies mirroring the standardization the larger phenomenon of globalization threatens. In establishing this series, our commitment is to provide support for complicated conversation within and across national and regional borders regarding the content, context, and process of education, the organizational and intellectual center of which is the curriculum.

SERIES EDITORS

Janet L. Miller, Teachers College, Columbia University (USA)
William F. Pinar, University of British Columbia (Canada)

INTERNATIONAL EDITORIAL ADVISORY BOARD

Alicia de Alba, National Autonomous University of Mexico

Shigeru Asanuma, Tokyo Gakugei University (Japan)

Tero Autio, Tallinn University (Estonia)

Bill Green, Charles Sturt University (Australia)

Manish Jain, Tata Institute of Social Sciences (India)

Lesley LeGrange, Stellenbosch University (South Africa)

Elizabeth Macedo, State University of Rio de Janeiro (Brazil)

José Augusto Pacheco, University of Minho (Portugal)

Zhang Hua, East China Normal University (China)

Reconsidering Canadian Curriculum Studies: Provoking Historical, Present, and Future Perspectives
Edited by Nicholas Ng-A-Fook and Jennifer Rottmann

Curriculum as Meditative Inquiry
By Ashwani Kumar

CURRICULUM AS MEDITATIVE INQUIRY

ASHWANI KUMAR

palgrave
macmillan

CURRICULUM AS MEDITATIVE INQUIRY
Copyright © Ashwani Kumar, 2013.

First published in 2013 by
PALGRAVE MACMILLAN®
in the United States—a division of St. Martin's Press LLC,
175 Fifth Avenue, New York, NY 10010.

Where this book is distributed in the UK, Europe and the rest of the world,
this is by Palgrave Macmillan, a division of Macmillan Publishers Limited,
registered in England, company number 785998, of Houndmills,
Basingstoke, Hampshire RG21 6XS.

Palgrave Macmillan is the global academic imprint of the above companies
and has companies and representatives throughout the world.

Palgrave® and Macmillan® are registered trademarks in the United States,
the United Kingdom, Europe and other countries.

ISBN: 978–1–137–32054–4

Library of Congress Cataloging-in-Publication Data

Kumar, Ashwani.
      Curriculum as meditative inquiry / Ashwani Kumar.
          pages cm.—(Curriculum studies worldwide series)
      ISBN 978–1–137–32054–4 (alk. paper)
          1. Education—Curricula—Philosophy. 2. Curriculum planning.
      3. Curriculum evaluation. I. Title.

LB1570.K78 2013
375′.001—dc23   2012043552

A catalogue record of the book is available from the British Library.

Design by Newgen Imaging Systems (P) Ltd., Chennai, India.

First edition: May 2013

10 9 8 7 6 5 4 3 2 1

Transferred to Digital Printing in 2013

For my mother, Shakuntla Verma,
who provides unconditional support to all my endeavors.

CONTENTS

A Note to the Readers

I have used endnotes frequently in this book. They are an essential part of the main text, explaining the text in more detail and suggesting further readings. Please pay close attention to the material included in the endnotes.

FOREWORD

I AM DELIGHTED TO INTRODUCE *CURRICULUM AS MEDITATIVE INQUIRY*, a book that steps out of conventional modes of inquiry to understand curriculum from a completely different vantage point. To consider curriculum as meditative inquiry implies a movement out of established discourses that pervade the extant literature and opens up new dimensions of inquiry and analyses. Our understanding of curriculum is usually in the context of the content of knowledge, or relationships between knowledge of different kinds, or disciplinary fields, and so on. In other words, curriculum is an object of analysis, a carefully crafted plan that lays out the charter for the educator and students. Ashwani Kumar however points to forms of individual and subjective engagement so that personal inquiry, autobiography, and reflexivity are all part of the process of being a part of the curriculum. Kumar's important book thus seeks to take us out of predetermined understandings of curriculum as given knowledge, which is valid, tested and established, and breaks new ground by taking as its focus an unexplored dimension of learning: the relationship between consciousness, meditative inquiry, and curriculum.

Kumar poses one of his three research questions as follows: "In what ways can we reimagine curriculum as a space for meditative inquiry that may provide self-transformative educational experiences to teachers and their students?" (this volume, 13). This question underlies Kumar's efforts to argue that human consciousness is the basis of all the structures that exist in society and unless there is an understanding of the many dimensions of this consciousness and how it works, the possibilities of transforming these structures remain remote and out of our grasp. At the heart of his effort to understand human consciousness and make it the focus of the curriculum, lie the works of the philosopher Jiddu Krishnamurti and the educator James Macdonald. Krishnamurti's perspective on learning, which transcends traditional forms of knowledge acquisition by compelling educators to help children to first understand themselves and their relationships; by allowing them to look, listen, observe, and thereby, to learn, is critical to Kumar's viewpoint. Taking a cue from Krishnamurti, Kumar contends that curriculum understood as meditative inquiry "emphasizes the significance of the art of awareness and the process of centering in order to have a deeper perception into one's own consciousness and one's relationships" (this volume, 125). This insight is crucial for understanding Kumar's project of *Curriculum as Meditative Inquiry*.

At the same time, Kumar's focus on consciousness is not embedded in any kind of individualistic or self-centered engagement with the curriculum. The focus therefore remains on "transformation" as an outcome of an education based on meditative inquiry. Kumar is also wary of "critical pedagogy" that advocates a change in the structures of domination that oppress people and society, and advocates instead the necessity for "awareness," self-reflection, and forms of understanding consciousness as ways of changing human relationships that are the basis of conflict and strife in society. Through processes of self-reflection and self-inquiry, based on constant awareness and observation, it is possible to bring about a change in consciousness and thereby in human relationships. Kumar's contention is that such change is possible only when educators can begin to look at curriculum in the context of consciousness. This is the crux of Kumar's argument that he persuasively draws out through the rest of the book.

The intensely personal nature of his exploration is courageous and is an innovative turn in the field of curriculum studies as social scientists rarely search for ways in which individual trajectories contribute to their professional lives and influence their research questions and agendas. There is a fear of "exposing" the most intimate aspects of one's being to professional colleagues as well as a fear of being accused of subjectivity in understanding social phenomena. Kumar confronts these fears by revealing precisely his inner journey in the context of his research questions and research agenda and lays bare his private journey as it is closely connected to the task he has undertaken in this book: to unravel the connections between human consciousness and human relationships that are so critical to maintaining balance and harmony in society.

The fact that the book is an exercise in building a theoretical framework about human consciousness and pedagogy without an empirical basis does not detract from its significance. It is in fact a major contribution to the field of curriculum studies in its initiation of an important theme for schooling today. In the same spirit, it is heartening to see how Kumar attempts to understand Krishnamurti's approach that looks to change in human consciousness as the route to social change alongside some other approaches that may not always be sympathetic to Krishnamurti's perspective. It is by building theoretical bridges and making connections across ideologies and discourses that Kumar offers a way out of the impasse that education, and indeed society, face today.

To remain limited within an information society that continues to expand, produce, and consume rapidly can only lead us to an end where there is no hope for renewal because "change" has become part of an ordinary existence. We are so used to technology and its advancement with knowledge and skills that support this growth that we look everywhere but within. We seek mastery of the external world because we assume that our control over it offers us a way out of our predicament as human beings. We need to take a breath and pause, and ask the question: Is there a future for our children in contemporary society torn as it is by strife, violence, and despair? Kumar's book shows us that the possibilities for such a future are based on an education that helps young people, as well as their teachers, to look inward to understand their relationship with society. Such an education may perhaps bring about a better way of living that is grounded in the mutual interpretation and understanding of one another's cultures and of being human in a swiftly changing world.

MEENAKSHI THAPAN
Professor of Sociology
Delhi School of Economics
University of Delhi

ROBERT SCHUMAN FELLOW (2012–2013)
European University Institute
Florence

Acknowledgments

I wish to extend my thanks to Professors Janet Miller and William Pinar for considering my book in the Curriculum Studies Worldwide series.

My heartfelt thanks goes to Professor William Pinar; without his support and encouragement, the publication of this book would not have been possible.

I extend my thanks to Professors Meenakshi Thapan and Karen Meyer for, respectively, writing a thoughtful Foreword and Afterword for my book.

I want to thank Martha Winterhalt, my student assistant at Mount Saint Vincent University, for making stylistic and editorial changes in my manuscript.

Finally, I want to thank Sarah Nathan, my editor at Palgrave, for her excellent support during the preparation of this manuscript.

SERIES EDITOR'S INTRODUCTION

ASHWANI KUMAR HAS RESPONDED TO THE CRISIS OF THE PRESENT by reminding us of the wisdom of the past, the wisdom of Jiddu Krishnamurti and James B. Macdonald. These public pedagogues appreciated that the ongoing crisis that is humanity requires us to confront questions of human consciousness. Krishnamurti knew that neither science nor finance—nor politics or religion—could resolve this crisis in any lasting way. Like Krishnamurti, Macdonald knew that heightened consciousness is the precondition of moral progress. Invoking the language of Marx, Macdonald argued that changing consciousness could precipitate structural change.

Meditative inquiry points us to passages through the opaque present. Such inquiry conveys the conviction that it is through the study of consciousness that one can come to understand human problems and act accordingly (see Mansbridge and Morris 2001). This is no narcissism, as Krishnamurti emphasized, no self-preoccupation but an ongoing observation of "life as a whole."[1] Situating this project historically, George Grant challenged us to "understand our technological destiny from principles more comprehensive than its own."[2] Indeed, for Grant "thought is steadfast attention to the whole."[3]

Attending to autobiographical or social experience is insufficient. Kumar thinks of Paulo Freire and his notion *of conscientization* or "critical consciousness." Critical consciousness (Kumar explains) "aims at developing the capacity to think in a way that does not blindly confirm to or accept the givens of the society." It is through critical—a form of heightened—consciousness that one comes to understand how one is implicated in what is. As Kumar conceives it, "Meditative inquiry is an existential process of being attentive to the way one thinks, feels, and acts inwardly as well as in one's relationship to people and nature." Indeed, "awareness implies a meditative state of mind," he continues, enabling a "deeper perception, communication, and learning, which are transformative in nature."[4]

In contrast to critical consciousness, or *currere*, meditative inquiry is, Kumar explains, no "reflexive-intellectual-critical engagement with self," but instead, he emphasizes, the "mere observation of it to experience its content directly, as it operates moment-to-moment." Kumar allows that "reflection, intellectual engagement, and critical thinking can be of immense value in order to understand self and its processes," but it is "the act of *pure observation*—without analysis or judgment— that provides an existential entry into one's innermost recesses." What is significant in meditation, Kumar concludes, is not the "analysis of the unconscious" but its "existential release." He writes, "When one allows the memory to surface in the meditative awareness, the mind, which is burdened with that memory, has free space, which is indicative of the 'transformation'."[5]

Kumar's reverberating work reactivates the past in curriculum studies, where almost 40 years ago the field in the United States grappled with questions of consciousness at a conference sponsored by the University of Rochester. At its most fundamental, I suggested in the preface to the proceedings (Pinar 1974b), sustained attention to consciousness represents a shift in the locus of attention from the observable to the inner life. Not that the Vietnam War or racial injustice or misogyny and homophobia disappear, but they—along with everything else—could now be discerned as outer forms, in some sense illusory. It was the American preoccupation with outer forms— "plastics" in that famous line from the movie *The Graduate*—that had provoked the 1960s efforts to experience heightened consciousness, as life lived only on the outside was, it seemed to many, especially young people, to be sterile. In education, this had meant—and still means— that educational research must be focused on the observable, on the quantifiable.

One of the keynote speakers at the 1973 University of Rochester conference was James B. Macdonald who, in his lecture, characterized technology as "an externalization of the hidden consciousness," what "humanity will eventually transcend...by turning inward" (1974, 91). "From this inward turn would come," Macdonald prophesized, "the rediscovery of human potential" (1974, 91). One of the "key processes in curriculum" (1974, 109) that Macdonald names is "meditative thinking," examining "the fundamental meaning of things" (1974, 110). Through the everlastingly significant work of Jiddu Krishnamurti and James B. Macdonald, Ashwani Kumar does just that.

WILLIAM F. PINAR

INTRODUCTION

> We are facing a tremendous crisis; a crisis which the politicians can never solve because they are programmed to think in a particular way—nor can the scientists understand or solve the crisis; nor yet the business world, the world of money. The turning point, the perceptive decision, the challenge, is not in politics, in religion, in the scientific world; it is in our consciousness. *One has to understand the consciousness of mankind [womankind], which has brought us to this point.*
>
> —Jiddu Krishnamurti (1983, 9; emphasis added)

> *[C]hange in human... consciousness is necessary and [a] precondition of a later political change....* If we utilize the concept of a dialectical relationship over longer periods of time between consciousness and structural change, it is at the "moment" of consciousness in this dialectic whereby we may expect to have any meaningful input in the change process.
>
> —James Macdonald ([1981a] 1995, 157; emphasis added)

Our world is in crisis. Our ecology, the foundation of life on planet earth, is in danger due to our lack of concern for the impact of our actions on the fragile ecosystem. Peace on earth is also denied because of antagonistic nationalistic, religious, ideological, racial, and economic groups. What is it that lies at the root of this crisis? Are all these issues and problems independent of each other? Or, is there a single source or root of all these problems with which our earth is plagued?

It is my understanding that most of our problems—psychological and collective—have their source in our consciousness, our very psychological nature. Take, for example, the issue of racial conflict. On the face of it, racial discrimination appears primarily to be a social, political, and economic problem. But, if one takes a deeper look, racial conflicts, which, no doubt, historically have been responsible for and resulted in economic exploitation and political oppression, are sustained and deepened through psychological processes of conditioning influences and identification. That is, the negative image about the "other" is constructed through an elaborate process of conditioning influences from the social, political, and religious organizations, on the one hand, and a search for belonging to a larger group through identification, on the other hand. In spite of the deeper psychological roots of racial problems, we primarily tend to focus on correcting them by means of political, economic, and legal measures. This tendency to focus on the outer or the structural aspect of a problem rather than grasping its psychological roots is the most predominant way of understanding and approaching problems in all spheres of life including the domain of education.

Since consciousness—the basis of thoughts, feelings, and actions— is the core of human existence, it is imperative that any fundamental change begins at the level of consciousness rather than structures. What do I mean by "structures" and "consciousness" and why do I think that a fundamental change in our structures cannot happen without a transformation in our consciousness? "Structures" basically mean all the things human beings have created; "consciousness" means the human psyche—comprising memories, psychological images, pleasures, pain, and fear—that is the source of all human thoughts, feelings, and actions. In my understanding, structures—social, political, and educational—are crystallized forms of consciousness. That is, whatever we, human beings, have produced on the face of the earth has to have a source in our consciousness. Thus, if we only focus on understanding the outer, or the structures, without considering the inner, or the consciousness, we are likely to remain confined to the surface manifestations of human conflicts and problems. In other words, if there were no human consciousness, there would not be any human structures. Furthermore, if there were no crisis in human consciousness, there would be no problems in our structures, at least of the insurmountable kind we are presently faced with. *Thus, in order to understand and transform our structures and what goes inside of them, it is essential that we understand and transform the consciousness that lies at their base.*[1]

This extraordinary significance of consciousness and the urgency of its transformation is at the core of the ideas of two individuals— Jiddu Krishnamurti and James Macdonald—whose works provide background material for this book. While coming from different backgrounds and standpoints, both men consider, as the epigraphs show, consciousness as the key to understanding and resolving human problems.[2] Krishnamurti was a world-renowned educator, philosopher, and institution builder from India who contributed immensely to the fields of philosophy, education, religious studies, consciousness studies, and psychology. His greatest contribution lies in his profound insights into the conflict-ridden nature of our consciousness and underscoring the significance of the art of awareness[3] to understand and transform the former. Macdonald was an important curriculum theorist whose pathbreaking scholarship laid the ground for the reconceptualization movement of curriculum studies—from "curriculum development" to "understanding curriculum"—in the United States (Pinar et al. 1995). Macdonald's most significant contribution to the field of education is his emphasis on the centrality of the "person in the curriculum" (Macdonald 1966b). Significantly, both Krishnamurti and Macdonald think that the highest function of education is to provide opportunities for teachers and their students to understand and transform their consciousness and thereby society. Consider their statements regarding the role of education:

> [Education] should help the student to recognize and break down in himself [herself] all social distinctions and prejudices, and discourage the acquisitive pursuit of power and domination. It should encourage the right kind of self-observation and the experiencing of life as a whole, which is not to give significance to the part, to the "me" and the "mine," but to help the mind to go above and beyond itself to discover the real. (Krishnamurti 1953, 46)

> [M]an [woman] has a personal, self-actualizing and creative capability not limited solely by biology or conditioning; that personal response is the avenue through which individuals stretch and reach their potentialities; and that a view of human development which wishes to focus upon human potentialities must centre upon the development aspect of personal responsiveness... [which, according to Gordon Allport (1955), constitutes]... "self-aware, self-critical and self-enhancing capacities." (Macdonald [1964]1995, 17)

In what ways can we provide opportunities in school so that students and their teachers "discover the real" and "reach their potential"? In other words, in what ways can we help lay the ground to provide self-transformative educational experiences in schools? By means of understanding curriculum as meditative inquiry, I propose.

Curriculum as meditative inquiry is a transformative approach to educational experience that aspires to help students and their teachers to deeply understand and, if possible, dissolve the conflicted nature of consciousness by cultivating a deeper sense of awareness.[4] It emphasizes *the arts of listening and seeing to have a deeper perception into one's own consciousness and one's relationships. It encourages the cultivation of the qualities of openness, aesthetics, and freedom in educational experience. Viewed from the perspective of meditative inquiry, education no more remains a problem of information transmission or means-end learning. On the contrary, it emerges as a space of freedom where the main focus is to learn about oneself and one's relationships with people, nature, and ideas.*[5] While there are several elements that contribute toward conceptualizing curriculum as meditative inquiry, "awareness" is its central dimension.

FOUR PERSPECTIVES ON AWARENESS: INFORMATION, CRITICISM, REFLECTION, AND MEDITATION

To understand the meaning and significance of awareness, I draw upon the works of Krishnamurti (2002, 2) who considers awareness to be "one of the greatest arts in life—perhaps the greatest." Before I discuss the way in which I have come to understand and view "awareness," or meditative inquiry,[6] I would like to discuss the three established ways in the field of education that invoke different views on what it means to be "aware." These three ways are information transmission, social criticism, and self-reflection.

Information transmission is the narrowest way of looking at the notion of awareness. In this perspective, making students aware is equal to transmitting disciplinary information to them in a passive and unproblematic manner without paying any attention to the political, cultural, and subjective dimensions of the educational process. Information transmission is another name for Tylerian rationality and is the core of the "curriculum development" paradigm that emerged with the publication of Franklin Bobbitt's *The Curriculum* (1918) and reached its zenith in Ralph Tyler's *Basic Principles of Curriculum and Instruction* (1949).

The information transmission view of education reduces teachers, students, and education to the level of instruments needed to achieve the predetermined and standardized goals set by administrators, politicians, and industrialists. Ralph Tyler' s *Basic Principles of Curriculum and Instruction* (organized around "objectives," "purposes," "experience," and "evaluation") as well as Frederick Taylor's (1911) *Principles of Scientific Management* (rooted in the scientific method of observation, precision, control, experimentation, and predictability) have served as the basic sources of theory and practice for those educators who consider passive transmission of information as the fundamental goal of education.

Theoretically, the information transmission perspective is dependent on positivism and behaviorism. Positivism, epistemologically speaking, considers truth as one, absolute, measurable, and uni-perspectival. Based on the method of empiricism, it denies anything that cannot be experienced through the senses. Thus it emphasizes objectivity and refuses to acknowledge the significance of cultural influences and subjective experiences. Likewise, behaviorism—that was primarily developed by the works of Edward Thorndike and Burrhus Frederic Skinner—emphasizes measurable aspects of knowledge and behavior and thereby focuses on memory-based learning and consequent behavior modification. Viewed from the lens of information transmission, which in turn is rooted in behaviorism, positivism, and scientism, curriculum is reduced to specified and attainable goals, textbook-centered instructions, and standardized assessments. Given the way in which most contemporary schools function in our society as "a degree factory, a credential provider, or a certifier" (Macdonald [1971a] 1995, 41), information transmission is the most dominant viewpoint to affect curriculum, teaching, and assessment.

Social criticism can be defined as the ability to be aware of and counter economic inequalities, gender and racial discriminations, religious orthodoxies, master narratives, and processes of normalization and regimes of truth. Central to social criticism is the idea that school knowledge—its selection, organization, and distribution—is political in nature and needs to be questioned and challenged to fight social injustices perpetuated in and through schools.

Social criticism is the core principle of "curriculum as political text" (Pinar et al. 1995). Curriculum as political text, variously known as reproduction theory, resistance theory, new sociology of education, and social reconstructionism, is one of the most prominent sectors of scholarship in contemporary curriculum theory. It primarily grew as a response to the atheoretical, apolitical, and ahistorical nature of the curriculum development paradigm that basically emphasizes a passive transmission of information. In its present form curriculum as political text is mainly known as critical pedagogy in North America.

Paulo Friere's (1973) notion *of conscientization* or "critical consciousness"—the ability to perceive social, political, and economic exploitation and take actions against the oppressive elements of social reality by means of a dialogical praxis to liberate the oppressed from oppressors and humanize the world where there would be no oppressor-oppressed contradiction—is the central idea of critical pedagogy. Critical consciousness aims at developing the capacity to think in a way that does not blindly confirm to or accept the givens of the society. It encourages students and teachers to question, analyze, denaturalize, decontextualize, and deconstruct the hegemonic political ideologies, religious superstitions and orthodoxies, sociocultural practices, and economic forces that have deeply permeated our consciousness. It also promotes inquiry into the deeper underlying meanings and ramifications of present societal characteristics such as exploitation, racial discrimination, gender inequalities, and income divides. Critical pedagogy's objective is social transformation, which is not possible if the givens of a society are taken for granted or remain unquestioned. In the absence of critical pedagogy, education is simply subject to pressures of the dominant political, economic, and cultural forces and serves as a passive agent of reproduction of the existing social reality. The critical pedagogy tradition developed from the works of Paulo Freire (1973, 1996a, 1996b, 1998), Henri Giroux (1981, 1983, 1989), Peter McLaren ([1994] 2006), and Joe Kincheloe (2003) among others, who primarily drew upon Marxist and neo-Marxist theories.

Self-reflection places emphasis upon developing the capacities of self-reflexivity and introspection to understand one's psychological, political, historical, and social situatedness. The enhanced understanding of one's self is also a step toward understanding the uniqueness of other individuals, their situatedness, and the resultant diversity of perspectives. Self-reflection, which aims at understanding the depth of one's subjectivity, forms the core of (auto)biographical studies. Conceptually, autobiographical theory finds its basis in psychoanalysis, phenomenology, and existentialism (Grumet 1976a, 1976b), as reflected by its emphasis on "individual history," "moment," "listening," and "what is." Autobiographical scholars criticize those sectors of curriculum scholarship, for example, traditionalists and critical pedagogues that undermine the significance of understanding the complexity of subjective consciousness and its relationship to social, political, and economic structures in educational inquiry.

Currere—the Latin root of curriculum meaning to run the course, the running of the course—is the central method of autobiographical theory that was devised by Pinar (1974a) and later elaborated by Pinar and Grumet (1976) to allow for a systematic study of "self-reflexivity" within educational process (Pinar 2004, 2012). "*Currere*," Grumet (1976b, 130–131) articulates, "is a reflexive cycle in which thought bends back upon itself and thus recovers its volition." The concept of currere abandons the static view of curriculum as a plan or document prepared by people in authority so that teachers and students may implement the former with as little subjective interference as possible. Currere, on the contrary, perceives curriculum to be a dynamic and subjective process whereby students and teachers—the real players in the educational process—can "study the relations between academic knowledge and life history in the interest of self-understanding and social reconstruction" (Pinar 2012, 44). In other words,

> [C]urrere seeks to understand the contribution academic studies makes to one's understanding of his or her life (and vice versa), and how both are imbricated in the society, politics, and culture. (Pinar 2012, 45)

The method of currere with its four steps or moments—regressive, progressive, analytical, and synthetical—characterizes "both temporal and cognitive movements in the autobiographical study of educational experience" (Pinar 2004, 35). In the regressive step one's past-lived experiences are considered the "data," which are generated through "free association"—a psychoanalytic technique—to revisit the past and thereby reexperience and "transform" one's memory. In the progressive step one looks at what is not yet and "imagines possible futures." The analytical stage is like phenomenological bracketing; in this step one examines the past and the future and creates a subjective space of freedom in the present. The present, the past, and the future are looked at as one movement. In the fourth, the synthetical moment, one revisits the "lived present" and being "conscious of one's breathing...one asks 'who is that?' Listening carefully to one's own inner voice in the historical and natural world, one asks: 'what is the meaning of the present?'... 'The moment of synthesis,' " Pinar (2004, 37) feels, "[is] one of intense interiority."

The method of currere, Pinar and Grumet (1976, vii) explain, "is a strategy devised to disclose experience, so that we may see more of it and see more clearly. With such seeing can come deepened understanding of the running, and with this, can come deepened agency." Currere abandons the anonymity and generalization characterizing positivistic research and emphasizes the primacy of the individual and what he or she "does with the curriculum, his active reconstruction of his passage through its social, intellectual, physical structures" (Grumet 1976b, 111).

Currere urges for an "intensified engagement with daily life" rather than "an ironic detachment" from it. This "intensified engagement" demands of those involved in educational experience to have "complicated conversations" within their own inner selves as well as within society to contribute to the projects of self-understanding and social reconstruction. Autobiography is concerned with reconstructing self and cultivating singularity, which is politically progressive and psychologically self-affirmative (Pinar, pers. comm.).

Awareness or meditative inquiry is an existential process of being attentive to the way one thinks, feels, and acts inwardly as well as in one's relationship with people and nature. Awareness implies a meditative state of mind wherein one listens to and observes people and nature without any interference from the constant movement of thought. Such meditative listening and observation allows for deeper perception, communication, and learning, which are transformative in nature. Consider Krishnamurti's own words from his book *Transformation of Man*:

> Is there an idea of awareness or is one aware? There is a difference. The idea of being aware, or *being* aware? "Aware" means to be sensitive, to be alive, to the things about one, to nature, to people, to color, to the

trees, to the environment, to the social structure...to be aware of all that is happening outwardly and to be aware of what is happening inside psychologically. ([1979] 2005, 215)

It is my contention that meditative inquiry points to something that is missing in the three existing conceptualizations—a deeper consideration of the nature of human consciousness and its complexity as well as the possibilities of its profound transformation. How is meditative inquiry different from the three existing conceptualizations in the field of education that invoke different meanings of the notion of "awareness"?

Information transmission is focused on information without any consideration of the consciousness of people involved in the educational experience. It is purely behavioristic, positivistic, and "scientific" in its orientation. Meditative inquiry, while not against information, is a profound existential approach to understanding one's consciousness. It is not an accumulation of information, but a learning of the nature of self and its relationship to people and nature.[7]

Critical pedagogy is entirely focused on social structures and has little place for consciousness.[8] The basic premise of critical pedagogy is that if, somehow, the social structures could be changed, all social problems will disappear on their own. But, what is society? Is not society the outcome of human relationships that are based on individuals and their interactions? If society is the outcome of human relationships, then, is not change in social structures an inevitable outcome of change in human relationships, which in turn must be based on change in individuals' consciousness? Social structures, for example, laws, can never be in constant revolution within themselves; whatever happens at the level of social structures is a modification that becomes static once carried out. Structures do not have a consciousness and thus cannot be self-reflective-conscious-critical. Individuals, in comparison to structures, can be in constant change within themselves for they do possess consciousness. If changing social structures transform individuals, then, we tend to believe that consciousness is the product of structures—an epiphenomenon—that can be shaped and directed in a particular way. If that is so, what is the difference between critical pedagogy and social engineering? Does not an epiphenomenal view of consciousness undermine the creative potential of human beings? *Can social change be truly possible or even desirable if the individuals themselves do not undergo transformation? Can there be peace and order in society if the individuals themselves are in conflict and disorder?*

Since critical pedagogy views social change as an outer-structural process and undermines the importance of consciousness in the manner I have discussed in this book, considering the significance of meditative inquiry is very important. Certainly, the conflicts and problems of the outer world are not independent of us and hence cannot be changed directly. It is essential for each individual to deeply understand how one, while being brought up in a social system ridden with conflicts and exploitation, acquires and inherits exploitative, acquisitive, and competitive tendencies, and perpetuates the fragmentation, conflicts, and degeneration of society. Such a profound understanding may not only help us break the repetitive and conditioned patterns inside our own selves but may also destroy the psychological roots of the exploitative and oppressive patterns in the society that operate through us. Obviously, the outer and the inner are not separate entities but work dialectically: the outer shapes the inner and vice versa and the chain continues. And, therefore, if only the outer world is changed without changing the inner life, the change will never be long lasting and radical. Awareness of one's own self—self-awareness— is as essential as an understanding of the outer reality. A change in the system or structure cannot lead to a real revolution for, such a change is a continuation of the same realities in a modified form. *Self-awareness is crucial; for, it is easy to hold others responsible for the misery of the world but it is hard to see oneself as an important component of such a degenerating process. Real revolution is the psychological revolution that comes about through self-awareness.*[9]

The key point of difference between meditative inquiry and currere is related to the central concern of the latter: self-reflexivity. Self-reflexivity encourages critical engagement with self, which instead of only being out-centered, turns inward to understand its complexity. Self-reflexivity however does not suggest existence of a state of mind where the perpetual movement of self—thoughts, experiences, and images—has come to a silence. *Awareness or meditative inquiry is not a reflexive-intellectual-critical engagement with self but a mere observation of it to experience its content directly, as it operates moment to moment.* Reflection, intellectual engagement, and critical thinking can be of immense value in understanding self and its processes, but it is, as I will explain later, the act of *pure observation*—without analysis or judgment—that provides an existential entry into one's innermost recesses. The approach in self-awareness is existential. If one observes oneself during daily activities such as bathing, putting on clothes, cooking, listening, and talking as well as watches the movement of one's thoughts and feelings without any interpretation or analysis, one consciously experiences the movement of the unconscious mind. In other words, awareness encounters the unconscious mind and dreams directly, independent of any analysis. The significant thing in meditation is not the analysis of the unconscious but its existential release that unburdens the mind of the psychological accumulations. When one allows memory to surface in meditative awareness, the mind, which is burdened with that memory, has free space, which is indicative of the "transformation."

In light of Krishnamurti's insights regarding "becoming" and "observer is the observed," it is also important to ask: who is regressing, progressing, analyzing, and synthesizing? The psychological process of *becoming* implies a psychological movement from "what is" to "what should be," which involves psychological time (Krishnamurti and Bohm 1985). While outwardly and structurally there is no problem in moving away from "what is" to "what should be" (e.g., the intention of converting a barren land into a garden is a valid process that involves thinking and chronological time), when it comes to a psychological movement involving psychological time to solve a psychological problem, for example, changing fear to non-fear, the movement from "what is" to "what should be" proves destructive. Why? Because *the observer is the observed*: the part of the thought that is fearful or angry (observed) and the part of the thought that wants to become fearless or non-angry (observer) are basically two aspects of one's thought. This psychological process of becoming—observer controlling the observed or ideal controlling the fact—is a separative process of thought that produces the illusion that the "observer" is different from the "observed" or the "thinker" is different from the "thought." When thought separates itself as the observer and the observed, there is a controller (e.g., the ideal of nonviolence) and the controlled (e.g., the fact of violence), which inevitably leads to suppression and conflict. When we look at ourselves with an ideal in mind, we have already gone against ourselves.

In the four steps of currere, it is of course the "I or Ego" that has separated itself from the whole movement of thought. I have briefly discussed the problem with this separation above and will elaborate later. Awareness adds a totally different dimension: *to observe without the observer*, that is, to observe the movement of thought without the interference of "I." In this observation there is no "I" that is observing, but only pure observation. Two things immediately happen when such observation happens even for a few seconds: there is a pure observation of the thing as it is and the separation or conflict, which is created through the Ego between itself and the object of observation, disappears. In my view, adding a fifth step to the method of currere—regressive-progressive-analytical-synthetical—*transcendental*, can steer the former in the direction of meditation. Transcendence implies an understanding that howsoever deep, Ego activity is superficial, limited, and conflict-ridden. This very understanding breaks the constant movement of the Ego and brings about transcendence, which, in turn, opens up the mind to intelligence and creativeness.[10]

While information, criticism, and reflection are important, in my view it is meditative inquiry that can be immensely helpful in understanding and transforming human consciousness and its conflicts. Curriculum as meditative inquiry is, I suggest, an approach to creating an environment that facilitates the development of awareness among teachers and their students. The central purposes of understanding curriculum as meditative inquiry include: a deep recognition that the nature of human consciousness is in crisis and that it affects and is, in turn, affected by the nature of contemporary educational institutions; a profound insight that the crisis of consciousness is existential in nature and hence demands an existential approach—meditative inquiry—for its comprehension and transformation; and a serious consideration of those activities and experiences—for example, the arts of listening, seeing, and dialogue—that give space to meditative inquiry in the educational process and thereby cultivate a sensitivity and awareness of one's self and one's relationship to people, nature, property, and ideas. *It is my contention that considering curriculum as meditative inquiry— that views consciousness, meditative inquiry, and curriculum as deeply connected spheres—can immensely help in broadening the horizons of educational theory and pedagogy.*

CENTRAL QUESTIONS

In this book I broadly engage with the following three questions:

In what ways do the characteristic features of human consciousness—fear, conditioning, becoming, and fragmentation—undermine self-awareness in educational experience?

What is meditative inquiry, and how can it help in cultivating awareness, which, in turn, can help in the understanding and transformation of human consciousness?

In what ways can we reimagine curriculum as a place for meditative inquiry that may provide self-transformative educational experiences to teachers and their students?

These questions primarily serve the purpose of understanding curriculum as meditative inquiry. More specifically, these questions facilitate an inquiry into the complex relationship of consciousness and education with particular reference to the factors of fear, conditioning, becoming, and fragmentation, and direct investigation into the role of meditative inquiry—an existential approach to understanding and transforming human consciousness—in the process of education.

A COMPLICATED CONVERSATION

Hermeneutically speaking, this work has grown out of an elaborate process of what Pinar (see 2004, 2012) enunciated as "complicated conversation." What brought about this "complicated conversation"? At a personal level, spiritual philosophers and mystics,[11] such as Kabir,[12] Krishnamurti, George Gurdjieff,[13] and Osho,[14] have touched me more profoundly than intellectuals. Not surprisingly, I am drawn to those intellectuals and philosophers who themselves were influenced by spiritual insights and mysticism, for example, David Bohm, Fritjoff Capra, Peter D. Ouspensky, Renee Weber, and Rupert Sheldrake, among others.

My preoccupation with spirituality and mysticism (not in a superficial and superstitious way) in general and my concern for the significance of self-awareness in educational process in particular provided a fertile ground for conceptualizing my work. For over ten years, and in a more concentrated manner in my work for the past seven years, I have had constant dialogues (textual and oral) with my teachers and friends that ranged in process and outcome from conflicting to extremely engaging and enriching. Had there been no dialogues, there would have been no book, at least of the nature it presently is. When I look backward in the river of time, I am able to identify major points or issues that brought about creative "tensionality" (see Aoki 2005) between my understanding and the dominant educational discourses in India and North America. It is as a result of the confrontations between my perspectives and the perspectives I encountered in educational literature that this book has come into being. What were/are these issues, concerns, or points?

The first significant point of tension is related to the *thinking and analysis* vis-à-vis *meditative inquiry*. It seems to me that from a Western perspective, thinking and analysis are the chief instruments of understanding and resolving psychological conflicts. However, if one observes closely the process of thought one realizes that it is beset with fear, becoming, conditioning, and fragmentation. That is, our thought or consciousness is fear-ridden, deeply conditioned, constantly moving between past and future, and is highly fragmented. In short, our consciousness is in a perpetual state of crisis. If this holds true then how can we be so sure that our thinking and analysis, which are based on the mechanism of thought, can solve our psychological problems? Our psychological problems, which are also at the root of our social problems, are existential—not theoretical or intellectual—and thus cannot be solved merely intellectually. We need an existential approach to meet the existential crisis, and that existential approach is *meditative inquiry*. This however does not mean that thinking and analysis are of no importance. They are, indeed, indispensable in the field of outward and structural reality as well as in communicating aspects of the psychological realm. But the problem starts when we try to understand and solve issues of our psychological sphere by blindly applying thinking and analysis.

The second point that invites complicated conversation is concerned with *subjectivity-as-self* vis-à-vis *subjectivity-as-awareness* and between *self-reflexivity* vis-à-vis *self-awareness*. Subjectivity-as-self limits subjectivity to the Ego or "I," which is a product of constantly moving images one has created about oneself and others based on one's physical, emotional, and psychological experiences. Subjectivity-as-self, which has been a subject matter of psychoanalysis, phenomenology, and existentialism, does not leave any opening for the presence of something deeper in human beings that is free of the constant movement of the Ego with its conflicts, contradictions, pains, and pleasures. Subjectivity-as-awareness points to something profound within us that remains unaffected from the turmoil of the self. Subjectivity-as-self invokes the methods of self-reflexivity and introspection that primarily aim at modifying the existing Ego. Subjectivity-as-awareness, on the contrary, requires choiceless awareness or pure observation of the mechanism of self without any judgment, analysis, comparison, or condemnation. It is the meditative inquiry, not never-ending analysis, that has the potential to have a profound perception of the nature of one's self and one's relationship to people, property, and ideas.

Another point of dissonance pertains to the relationship between *structure* vis-à-vis *consciousnesses* and between *political revolution* vis-à-vis *psychological revolution*. This can also be considered a difference between Eastern perceptions of reality and Marxist conceptualizations. While it is almost impossible to determine with certitude which of the two—structure or consciousness—is more important, it is not very difficult to see their implications if we are ready to hypothetically discuss the two possible options. If we say that it is the structures that have produced consciousness or consciousness is an epiphenomenon, as is accepted in Marxist theory, we enter a very dangerous path detrimental to human freedom and growth. Considering structures of primary importance implies that human beings can be organized and controlled like machines. They are of value as long as they fit the blueprint of a utopia-like structure. A structure-oriented perspective, naturally, demands political revolution along preestablished theories. In this viewpoint are present the seeds of totalitarian and authoritarian ways of dealing with human beings and their problems. Contrary to the structural perspective is the perception that views structures as crystallized forms of consciousness. According to the latter view, if our structures are exploitative and violent, it is because of our psychological nature. This view demands a psychological revolution wherein what becomes the focus of transformation is not the society and its structures, but individual subjectivities, which, in actuality, through their interactions, form society.

In addition to the points I have discussed above, the critical reflections of my teachers (especially my PhD supervisor, Professor William Pinar), my colleagues, and friends[15] on my work have contributed immensely to the writing of this book. Most of the questions, and my responses to them, that the readers will come across throughout this book are a testimony to the enactment of, on my part, a complicated conversation that was extremely fruitful to my own personal development and learning.

OVERVIEW OF THE CHAPTERS

The "Introduction" provides the rationale for my work, discusses the four perspectives on the notion of "awareness," lists key questions, and articulates the complicated conversation as a hermeneutical process that guided the writing of this book.

Chapter 1, "Krishnamurti, Macdonald, and Myself" provides brief biographical sketches of Krishnamurti and Macdonald whose works have greatly influenced my conceptualization of curriculum as meditative inquiry. In addition, I also share my reflections about relevant people, events, and experiences in my own personal history, which, in many ways, have inspired me to write this book. I conclude this chapter with identifying the four principles of understanding curriculum as meditative inquiry, each of which I will discuss in detail in the next four chapters.

Chapter 2, "On the Nature of Consciousness" explains in detail the four characteristic features of human consciousness—fear and insecurity, conditioning influences and image-making, becoming and psychological time, and fragmentation and conflict—that are at the very root of individual and social conflicts. More specifically, it explicates how fear and insecurity are responsible for inequalities of wealth, nationalistic and religious antagonism, and various sorts of discriminations; the ways in which conditioning influences and image-making bring about divisiveness within and between people; how becoming as a psychological process from "what is" to "what should be" leads to psychological conflicts and dissipation of energy; and in what ways fear, becoming, and conditioning are responsible for fragmentation and conflict at all levels of the individual psyche and the society it has created.

Chapter 3, "On the Nature of Education" sheds light upon the ways in which the general characteristic features of consciousness are reflected in and perpetuated through educational institutions by means of creating and sustaining fear among children through imposing authority and discipline and seeking conformity; conditioning children's minds through political and religious propaganda; fueling the process of becoming by way of cultivating ideology of achievement and ideals; and bringing about fragmented personality structures by overemphasizing cognitive learning at the expense of bodily, emotional, creative, and spiritual aspects of children's beings.

Chapter 4, "On the Nature of Meditative Inquiry" on the one hand, points out the limitations of thinking, analysis, system, and authority in understanding and transforming human consciousness and, on the other hand, emphasizes the possibilities of meditative inquiry as an existential approach to perceive and transform our consciousness and its conflicts.

Chapter 5, "On the Nature of Curriculum as Meditative Inquiry" discusses the basic elements—personal responsiveness, openness, aesthetics, freedom, love, transcendence, awareness, and centering—that may guide us to reimagine curriculum as a space for meditative inquiry. Curriculum as meditative inquiry undermines the factors of fear, becoming, conditioning, and fragmentation in the educational process, on the one hand, and, on the other hand, cultivates teachers' and students' potential for self-understanding and self-transformation.

The "Conclusion" summarizes the book, states its major contributions to the field of curriculum studies in particular and education in general, articulates its limitations, and suggests directions for future inquiry.

CHAPTER 1

KRISHNAMURTI, MACDONALD, AND MYSELF

INTRODUCTION

This book has emerged as a result of my engagement with the profound works of Jiddu Krishnamurti and James Macdonald. There are three aspects of their ideas that provided a strong foundation to understanding curriculum as meditative inquiry. First, both men consider the individual—not systems, theories, methods, plans, or tests—to be the core of education. In their view the highest function of education is to provide grounds for self-understanding and self-transformation. Second, both of them recognize the deleterious effects of conditioning influences, fear, discipline, authority, and fragmentation on the growth and development of children, on the one hand, and the positive role of listening, dialogue, and understanding for transformative teaching and learning, on the other hand. Both Krishnamurti and Macdonald consider individual and social change as inseparable processes. While they recognize the urgent need for social transformation, they think that the most significant role education can play is to provide opportunities to teachers and their students so that they may understand their consciousness and transform it, which, in turn, will transform society. Given their tremendous contribution to my research as well as due to a general lack of knowledge about their lives and works in education literature, I provide brief biographical introductions about them in this chapter. I also provide a brief autobiographical statement to recognize significant people and ideas, including Krishnamurti and Macdonald, who, in many ways have inspired my thinking and practice as a human being and an educator.

JIDDU KRISHNAMURTI: TRUTH IS A PATHLESS LAND

Jiddu Krishnamurti (1895–1986)—a widely regarded philosopher, educator, and institution builder—was born to a Hindu Brahmin family in Madanapalle, India on May 12, 1895. At the age of 14 he was "discovered" to have a "unique aura that contained no selfishness" by a theosophist and psychic, Charles Leadbeater (Jayakar 1986, 24). Subsequently, Krishnamurti was adopted by Annie Beasent, the then president of the Theosophical Society,[1] who was also an ardent social reformer and participant in India's struggle for independence from the British Raj. In 1911, at the age of 16, Krishnamurti was taken to England where he was to be educated and prepared to be a "vehicle" for the arrival of the Lord Maiterya, the "World Teacher." For his entire adolescence and youth, theosophists prepared Krishnamurti as the "vehicle" for the arrival of the "World Teacher," which certainly involved a strictly disciplined life. However, Krishnamurti reported later that although he was being conditioned heavily by the theosophists, in his innermost self he was going through a silent revolution (Jayakar 1986; Lutyens 1990). He was constantly questioning all kinds of beliefs and rituals, orthodoxies and superstitions, authority and hierarchy.

At the age of 27 in 1922, Krishnamurti went through a "life changing" experience at Ojai Valley, California involving severe pain in his back and brain for several days. His biographer and close friend, Pupul Jayakar (1986, 47), describes the process as the awakening of *Kundalini* energy.[2] His experience completely disillusioned Krishnamurti of the place of any authority in psychological and religious matters. In 1929, at the age of 33, Krishnamurti dissolved the "Order of the Star in the East,"[3] which he was a president of and declared:

> I maintain that Truth is a pathless land, and you cannot approach it by any path whatsoever, by any religion, by any sect. That is my point of view, and I adhere to that absolutely and unconditionally. Truth, being limitless, unconditioned, unapproachable by any path whatsoever, cannot be organized; nor should any organization be formed to lead or to coerce people along any particular path. (Krishnamurti 1929)

In essence, Krishnamurti maintained throughout his life what he said in his "Dissolution Speech." This speech was a paradigm shift that shook the entire theosophical society including Annie Besant. This speech was the beginning of the enfoldment of the unique teachings that were completely bereft of any organized belief and a sense of authority and for which Krishnamurti is respected by people the world over including theosophists. However, at the time of the dissolution of the order theosophists disliked such a decision on the part of Krishnamurti who they were preparing to become their "Teacher." Annie Beasent, who considered Krishnamurti her son, was extremely worried about the future of Krishnamurti for she believed that he knew nothing of the way the world works. On her request a few theosophists left the Theosophical Society and took the responsibility to take care of the social life of Krishnamurti. For the next few years Krishnamurti went into complete isolation in Ojai Valley, California.

It was after World War II that Krishnamurti's teachings began to take shape. He traveled throughout the world engaging common people, scholars, teachers, and students in a dialogical encounter regarding the need to recognize the crisis in human consciousness and the urgency of its transformation to create a peaceful world. He maintained a thoroughly original perception into life's numerous problems. He declared that he was nobody's teacher but a "simple man" who wants to point toward something "sacred" in life, untouched and uncontaminated by thought. This "sacred" one may call "Truth," "God," or "Reality," which one has to discover within one's own self through constant awareness of one's behavior, thoughts, and emotions and one's relationship to people and nature.

In his lifetime Krishnamurti traveled worldwide and spoke for over 60 years on vital issues concerning the future of humanity and published over 70 books. During the last 40 years of his life, on average, Krishnamurti gave a hundred talks every year (Martin 1997). Broadly, his works are comprised of his authored texts, talks, question and answer series, and dialogues. Some of his important works include *First and the Last Freedom* (1954) (with a magnificent foreword by Aldous Huxley), *Education and the Significance of Life* (1953), *The Ending of Time* (1985) (which is collection of his dialogues with theoretical physicist David Bohm), *A Wholly Different Way of Living* (2000) (which is a collection of his dialogues with Professor

Allan W. Anderson of San Diego State University), three volumes of *Commentaries On Living*, and *Collected Works* (Vol. 1–17). Major themes that characterize Krishnamurti's writings, public talks, and dialogues with students, teachers, and scholars include education, meditation, fear, self-knowledge, psychological revolution, world crisis, peace, truth, intelligence, consciousness, time, and creativity.

During the 1950s while North American curriculum theory and school education was still working under the dominance of Ralph Tyler's *Basic Principles of Curriculum and Instruction* (1949) and serving the demands of industrialization, militarization, and consumerism, Krishnamurti by means of his *Education and the Significance of Life* (1953) had already critiqued the nature and character of a positivistic, behavioristic, and capitalistic, or more succinctly, materialistic education, centered on the principles of reward and punishment and technical efficiency. Krishnamurti's insights into the nature and purpose of education are contained in more than ten books.[4] Of them, he authored three (*Education As Service*, 1912; *Education and the Significance of Life*, 1953; and *Whole Movement of Life is Learning: J. Krishnamurti's Letters to His Schools*, 2006)[5] while others[6] are based on his dialogues and talks with students, teachers, parents, and scholars. As an institution builder, Krishnamurti established several schools, study centers, and foundations in India, the United Kingdom, and the United States of America that continue to survive as one of the most significant alternative educational institutions in the world.[7] By means of his writings and talks, dialogues with people the world over, and through establishing alternative schools and study centers, Krishnamurti shared a significant vision of education.

On the one hand, Krishnamurti's vision of education criticizes modern educational institutions that cultivate in children fear through emphasizing discipline, authority, and conformity; instill the poison of ambitions and competitiveness; influence delicate minds with destructive conditioning; and create a deep-rooted fragmented personality structure. On the other hand, his life's work lays the foundation of a "right kind of education," which, instead of fear, becoming, conditioning, and fragmentation, nurtures meditative inquiry or awareness of one's thoughts, emotions, and actions to bring about self-knowledge and thereby psychological and social transformation.

Krishnamurti influenced people worldwide including physicists (David Bohm, Fritjof Capra, and George Sudarshan), authors (Mary

Cadogon, Joseph Campbell, Howard Fast, Kahlil Gibran, Aldous Huxley, Iris Murdoch, Henry Miller, George Bernard Shaw, and Alan Watts), biologists (Jonas Salk, Rupert Sheldrake, and Maurice Wilkins), psychiatrists (Hedda Bolgar, Ruben Feldman-Gonzalez, John Hidley, David Shainberg, and Benjamin Weinniger), philosophers (Allan W. Anderson, Nalini Bhushan, Raymond Martin, Jacob Needleman, Walpola Rahula, Ravi Ravindra, Hillary Rodrigues, Eugene Schallert, Huston Smith, and Renee Weber), creative artists (Sidney Field, Anta Loos, Michael Mendizza, Van Morrison, Alan Rowlands, Leopold Stokowski, and Beatrice Wood), and educators (Scott Forbes, Krishan Kumar, Karen Meyer, Jack Miller, Jane Piirto, and Meenakshi Thapan), among others.[8] Toward the end of his life Krishnamurti was also invited to deliver a lecture at the United Nations in the year 1984[9] and was awarded a UN Peace Medal. Krishnamurti died of pancreatic cancer on February 17, 1986 in Ojai Valley, California.[10]

JAMES MACDONALD: PERSON IN THE CURRICULUM

James Bradley Macdonald, the "great curriculum theorist" (Pinar 2009c, 190), was born on March 11, 1925, to a prominent family in Delavan, Wisconsin.[11] Macdonald's father's engagement with "intellectually stimulating activities" and his mother's "strong beliefs about fairness and equality and justice which she constantly communicated to her children" (Burke 1985, 87) had a strong impact on Macdonald's life, as is explicit from his own intellectual vitality and emphasis on social justice and change.

Macdonald's formal schooling began earlier than intended due to the untimely death of his older sister. While he was a good student, he was constantly reminded at school that he was not scoring as high grades as his sister did or as his potential indicated. Macdonald considered these views "stupid." Instead of worrying about grades he "involved himself in many activities [drama, football, and social contacts] that were interesting and exciting" (Burke 1985, 86). This explains Macdonald's abhorrence of technological rationality, "ideology of achievement" (Macdonald [1971b] 1995) or "accumulative consumptive psychology of schools" (Macdonald [1975c] 1995), on the one hand, and his appreciation of "openness," "aesthetics," and "playfulness" (Macdonald [1964] 1995), on the other hand.

Macdonald's higher education began with his admission into Whitewater State University in Whitewater, Wisconsin as an engineering major. Macdonald had to leave his studies and join the Navy after just one semester due to World War II. It was during his posts in Guinea and the Philippines that Macdonald resisted against racism in the military, especially toward blacks, and concluded that much of the military was "bureaucratic idiocy" (Burke 1985, 90)! No doubt it was during his years in the military that Macdonald learnt about the problems of bureaucratic, disciplinary, hierarchical, and authoritative organizations. How schools act, in many ways, as military organizations is explicit in his many writings (Macdonald [1971a] 1995).

After returning from the war on G. I. Bill, Macdonald rejoined college as a history and sociology major with a minor in political science. Macdonald greatly enjoyed history classes because they provided him with the "opportunity to explore the background of events, to think about relationship, and to wonder" (Burke 1985, 90). Macdonald was deeply influenced by a sociology professor who taught a class of five hundred students. Macdonald was amazed with his ability to probe deeply and invite students to probe further in such an enormous classroom. Contrary to his experiences in history and sociology, he abhorred a professor of economics who dictated notes from his notebook (Burke 1985). In my understanding, it is here that Macdonald realized the problems of behaviorist approaches to teaching, on the one hand, and the significance of "person in the curriculum" and "meditative thinking," on the other hand, which are reflected all through his writings.

Macdonald took his first education course with Professor John Rothney, who emphasized a holistic approach to understanding the relationship among cognitive, affective, and social domains. This course was transformative for Macdonald in many ways. He learnt many problematic aspects of the public education system, such as the unrestrained use of authority and its dehumanizing effects on students and teachers (Burke 1985). These concerns are apparent in his vision of education that he developed later as a curriculum theorist.

While four years in college earned Macdonald a secondary teaching certificate, he knew, based on his school teaching experience, that the profession was not a best fit for him. He realized that the teachers and students were primarily concerned with grades rather than subject matter. Disillusioned, Macdonald seriously considered studying sociology in graduate school. However, due to a half-hour-long engaging conference with Professor Virgil Herrick, director of a new program in the area of elementary education at the University of Wisconsin in Madison (UWM), Macdonald was convinced that he should remain in the field of education. After a year of teaching as a fourth grade teacher in a school in Park Forest (Illinois) where he enjoyed good relationships with parents, and served as an elected chairman of the local chapter of the National Education Association, Macdonald returned to Madison to finish his Master's degree and, subsequently, joined the doctoral program in the same university (Burke 1985).

Doctoral studies at the UWM was pivotal for Macdonald in many ways. He enjoyed a rich learning environment where many dimensions of curriculum, teaching, and learning were discussed and debated. It was also here that Macdonald found his lifelong friend and colleague, Dwayne Huebner. Both Macdonald and Huebner, who according to Pinar et al. (1995) were two major figures of the curriculum reconceptualization movement in North America, inspired each other's thinking and writing. Both of them worked under the supervision of Virgil Herrick, who they highly regarded. Notably, Macdonald did his doctoral dissertation—"Some Contributions of a General Behavior Theory for Curriculum" (1956)—in the tradition of positivistic research, a tradition against which he himself fought later in his distinguished career.

Macdonald's first university appointment was as assistant professor in Curriculum and Extension at the University of Texas-Austin where he worked during 1956–1957. Being here, Macdonald was influenced by special education classrooms that embodied significant aspects of a progressive education, such as, valuing and respecting individual needs and an open and caring environment. It was in these classrooms that Macdonald thought "good liberal education" (Burke 1985, 97) was taking place.

From 1957–1959, Macdonald worked at New York University. He was invited there to direct a graduate program to certify elementary education teachers, to design effective methods of teacher preparation, and to teach foundation courses in education. While in New York, Macdonald published his first article: "Practice Grows from Theory and Research" (1958). In this article, Macdonald primarily "focused on the link between the behavioral sciences and education, and encouraged a concerted effort to synthesize and test a large framework" (Burke 1985, 97). This article represents the beginning of the period of what he calls "scientific thinking" in his career.[12] What is however interesting is, as pointed out by Burke (1985, 98), that "even in this very early technical writing... Macdonald identified the self as a source of important knowledge which has an impact upon the total teaching/learning experience." "Better teaching practices," Macdonald (quoted in Burke 1985, 98) emphasized, "come from better sources of knowledge. Personal experience is one source of knowledge." While Macdonald continued to work in the behaviorist tradition for several more years, he began to realize that "purely scientific research excluded the aspects of feeling and affect."

This realization regarding the limitations of instrumental rationality in the educational sphere further deepened due to a number of factors. First, Macdonald was invited as an associate professor to direct the Campus Laboratory School and the School of Experimentation and Research at the University of Wisconsin, Milwaukee in 1959. Here Macdonald got the opportunity to work with individuals and groups of students. At UWM, Macdonald also collaborated with Professor Ethel Kunkle and Barbara Bixby, the Campus School kindergarten teachers, on a study of the junior kindergarten experience in the campus school (Spodek 1985). Second, between 1960 and 1966, Macdonald served and later directed the Research Commission of the Association for Supervision and Curriculum Development. A significant part of the commission was its biannual research institutes where scholars from diverse areas, such as, anthropology, psychology, and sociology, gathered to discuss and debate issues of educational importance. Macdonald found these institutes highly intellectually stimulating. Finally, during this period, Macdonald served as a university representative to the Lakeshore Curriculum Council that directed a study of individualized reading programs in eight school systems. This program basically contributed to understanding the importance of social and humanistic psychological perspectives in education. These factors provided humanistic underpinnings to Macdonald's work from the mid-1960s onward, starting with his very important essay—"An Image of Man: The Learner Himself" ([1964] 1995; Burke 1985). In this essay, drawing upon psychoanalytical and humanistic approaches, Macdonald underscored the importance of "personal responsiveness," "openness," and the "reality-centered school" to provide the basis for an education aimed at self-actualization. Macdonald further explained his concerns for the "primacy of the particular" (Pinar 2009a) in three other significant essays: "Learning, Meaning and Motivation: An Introduction" (1966a), "Person in the Curriculum" (1966b), and "A Proper Curriculum for Young Children" (1969). Macdonald's concerns for the "person" were reflected in the field of curriculum during the 1970s and since then in subjectivity-oriented scholarships in curriculum theory, which includes autobiographical, holistic, humanistic, theological, psychoanalytical, phenomenological, and existentialist approaches. This emphasis on the "person" was rooted in Macdonald's love for children. Remembering Macdonald's life and works, Dwayne Huebner (1985, 28), one of his closest friends and colleagues, reflects on Macdonald's chief concern as an educator:

> Jim loved children. That is one of several reasons he became an elementary school teacher. It was this love that made him aware of the limits of the curriculum, the limits of teachers, and the limits of schooling. He loved kids enough not to give up on teachers, curriculum, or schools. He spent his life redeeming them—bringing teachers, curriculum, and schools to the point where they would serve children rather than entrap them. This was his work.

During the 1970s, Macdonald's writings began to show signs of sociopolitical humanism. This change was necessitated by the political events like the Vietnam War and the civil rights movement. The demand of the political situation was combined with Macdonald's expanding intellectual horizons as well as his childhood education from his mother regarding the importance of social justice and fairness. While Macdonald became increasingly interested in understanding the negative influences of political, cultural, and economic systems on schooling, he, unlike political scholars of curriculum theory who overstressed structures at the expense of individual subjectivity (see Pinar 2009b; Pinar et al. 1995), never neglected the centrality of the individual in educational process. "When I moved to social humanism," Macdonald told Burke (1985, 106), "I took the personal with me, of course." In an autobiographical statement, Macdonald (1975a, 3) summarizes the centrality of the personal and the social in his life's works:

> Personally, my own work in the field in retrospect is best explained to myself as an attempt to combine my own personal growth with a meaningful social concern that has some grounding in the real world

of broader human concerns. Thus, education has served as a societal pivotal point to explore myself and the broader human condition in a meaningful context.

Macdonald's major papers that reflect his sociopolitical concerns include "The School as a Double Agent" ([1971a] 1995); "Curriculum and Human Interest" ([1975b] 1995); "The Quality of Everyday Life in Schools" ([1975c] 1995); "Living Democratically in School: Cultural Pluralism" ([1977a] 1995); "Curriculum as a Political Process" (undated; published in 1995 in *Theory As A Prayerful Act: The Collected Essays of James B. Macdonald*); and "Curriculum, Consciousness, and Social Change" ([1981a] 1995).[13] These papers, in certain ways, reflect the beginning of understanding "curriculum as political text," a sector of curriculum scholarship that emerged in the 1970s and continues to remain important in the contemporary field (Pinar et al. 1995). Significantly, along with enriching the field with his theoretical contributions, Macdonald also worked in the area of curriculum development that is "embodied in the University of North Carolina at Greensboro and the University of Milwaukee Social Studies Project . . . that addressed social problems and that encouraged students to identify their own values through a method of critical inquiry" (Burke 1985, 112).

In 1966 Macdonald became professor at the UWM where, later on, he was promoted as the director of Doctoral Studies and chairperson of the Department of Curriculum. In 1972 Macdonald left UWM to join the University of North Carolina at Greensboro (UNCG) as Distinguished Professor of Education. It was during his tenure at the UNCG that Macdonald's writing took a transcendental turn. One of his most significant essays that appeared during this period was "A Transcendental Developmental Ideology of Education" ([1974] 1995). In this essay Macdonald critiqued the four preexisting ideologies— romantic, developmental, cultural transmission, and radical—and argued for the importance of transcendental ideology. In this essay Macdonald introduced many crucial concepts—"transcendence," "centering," "meditative thinking," "education for perception," "personal knowledge," and "tacit dimension"—that were probably completely new to the curriculum audience. In my view, this essay is the most significant contribution of Macdonald to curriculum theory and practice and to my own research.

A major contribution of Macdonald's scholarship to curriculum theory in particular and education in general was his strong faith in the transformative power of curriculum. Disagreeing with Joseph Schwab (1970) and Dwayne Huebner (1976) who declared the field of curriculum "moribund," Macdonald ([1977b] 1995, 138) professed, "[I]f curriculum is moribund then society as we know it is also moribund." In other words, *moribundity of curriculum is the moribundity of society itself.* He explains,

> Curriculum, it seems to me, is the study of "what should constitute a world for learning and how to go about making this world." As such it implies, in microcosm, the very questions that seem to be of foremost concern to all of humanity. Such questions as "what is the good society, what is a good life, and what is a good person," are implicit in the curriculum. (137)

The normative focus of Macdonald's work reached its apex when he urged educators to view curriculum "theory as a prayerful act." According to Macdonald ([1981b] 1995),

> The act of [curriculum] theorizing is an act of faith, a religious act. It is the expression of belief, and as William James [1917] clearly expounds in *The Will To Believe,* belief necessitates an act of the moral will based on faith. *Curriculum theorizing is a prayerful act.* It is an expression of the humanistic vision of life. (181)

Indeed, it is for the realization of this "humanistic vision of life" that Macdonald devoted his work as an educator. Macdonald was not naively optimistic, but realistically hopeful. Invoking Fromm's (1968) emphasis on "hope," Macdonald ([1981a] 1995) urges us:

> We must, as Erich Fromm [1968] says, keep up our hope; which he defines as the willingness to keep working for what we believe in with the full realization that we may never see it come to fruition in our lifetime. (170)

Macdonald died in 1983 at the relatively young age of 58 due to kidney failure. Macdonald's significant contribution to curriculum theory was celebrated at the 1984 Conference on Curriculum Theory and Practice at Bergamo on November 2, 1984, which was organized in his honor (Apple 1985; Burke 1985; Grumet 1985; Huebner 1985; Molnar 1985; Pinar 1985; Spodek 1985; Wolfson 1985a, 1985b). Bradley J. Macdonald has posthumously published his father's most influential essays in *Theory As A Prayerful Act: The Collected Works of James B. Macdonald.*

AUTOBIOGRAPHICAL ROOTS OF CURRICULUM AS MEDITATIVE INQUIRY

This work is rooted in my personal history. As I briefly explained previously, in my intellectual journey I have faced significant challenges from the academic world as well as from within myself in bringing together my academic pursuits and inner life. The inward challenge was grounded in my intention to keep the "inner work" separate from my academic life. Academically, for about eight years from 1997—while I was in my second year of an undergraduate program in Geography at the University of Delhi[14] and when I read the first book on the subject of meditative inquiry, *Dhyan Sutra* (*Principles of Meditation*)[15] (Osho 1989)—through 2004 when I finished my Master of Philosophy in Geography (MPhil), neither was there a possibility in the institutional setting nor was there a strong inward desire to incorporate my personal search into my intellectual pursuits.

While I enjoyed learning geography at Kirori Mal College during my undergraduate years due to the presence of Professor K. K. Mojumdar, the five years I spent thereafter to study geography further at Delhi School of Economics were not very productive. I was so totally discontented with what was going on in the Department of Geography—information transmission without much critical engagement—that I almost withdrew myself from academic participation.[16] When I did participate, it was primarily to criticize what was going on in the name of education. The reason why I continued my studies in the Department of Geography was rather pragmatic: in order to become a university professor, which was my dream career, it was necessary that I complete a Master's degree. Since I was unable to pass the National Educational Test[17]—a national level exam to determine the eligibility of a candidate to become a university professor!— I registered myself in a Master of Philosophy program in the same department. Interestingly, it was during this period that my search to understand the meaning of life intensified.

Thanks to two of my friends—Anurag Baliyan and Rajeev Kumar[18]—and Professor Mojumdar[19] who would intelligently and passionately engage with me with the same intensity to find out or inquire as the character Gurdjieff would ask in the movie, *Meetings with Remarkable Men*[20]: "Why am I here?" I need to say at this point that in no way am I trying to portray myself as somebody special. I was going through—I am still going through—a crisis of the consciousness as anybody else, but there was/is always this flame somewhere that this crisis cannot be the end of life. The main reason behind writing these autobiographical reflections is to underscore how one's life history shapes one's intellectual and existential pursuits and why it is important to have harmony in one's inner and outer activities.

With this discontented and critical frame of mind and due to financial requirements, but without any desire to teach in a school— as I always wanted to be a university professor after I got over the desire to be a government administrator, which is a powerful, stable, and economically rewarding career—I took up a job as a high school geography teacher in Apeejay School, Pitampura, which is a private and privileged English language school in New Delhi. While I had been critical of the educational system for sometime due to my readings of Osho's work, it was during this job that I had firsthand experience of the deleterious impacts of modern education on the growth and development of children and teachers.

I loved my students—not that I did not become angry and scold them at times—and enjoyed teaching, especially when I was able to encourage children to have debates and discussions in the class. But I absolutely hated the administrative hierarchy and textbook-driven curriculum. I noted an absence of critical engagement on the part of most of my colleagues due to a lack of desire, administrative control, and pressure of exams. I also observed that parents pressured their children and teachers so that the former might score high grades. Good performance in exams was most important, even when it meant undermining children's talents. Pursuing one's talent was permissible as long as it did not interfere with the "real" education leading to the choice of a profession that pays well. Teachers were busy implementing a state/management-mandated curriculum without any critical engagement. Students were trying to please teachers and parents by doing the best they could to memorize the information and reproduce it in exams. Those students who would not fit into the system would be punished, subtly or explicitly, without any serious consideration of their perspectives.

Since I taught without a teaching certificate, I was advised by D. K. Bedi,[21] the principal of my school, to complete a Bachelor of Education degree (BEd) to get a permanent job at the school. While I had no desire to go back to school, I decided to take the BEd entrance examination on the strong recommendation from my MPhil supervisor, Professor B. Khan, who thought that since I was unable to pass the National Educational Test, in order to have job security it was important to have a BEd degree. With extreme reluctance I took the entrance exam and to my complete surprise I passed it and joined the Central Institute of Education (CIE) in July 2005.

Within a week at CIE I realized somewhere in the depth of my heart that I have found my real vocation. For the first time in my life, I found myself in an institutional setting where I was able to discuss, at least to some extent, what I have been studying and discussing outside the mainstream curriculum. I also found many books by Krishnamurti in the CIE library. While I had tried to read Krishnamurti before, I found it hard to understand his in-depth explorations into the nature of human consciousness. It was not until I joined CIE that I studied Krishnamurti with serious attention and with greater comprehension. I was greatly intrigued by the directness and lucidity with which Krishnamurti explained his insights and engaged his audience in the process of a dialogical learning about the nature of self. I thoroughly enjoyed—not only intellectually but also deeply—reading and experimenting with his insights regarding the nature of consciousness and meditation.

Nevertheless, my study of Krishnamurti's work was more or less solitary at CIE, where professors, generally speaking, were more interested in constructivism and critical pedagogy with a particular focus on the ideas of John Dewey, Jean Piaget, Paulo Freire, Michael Apple, Henry Giroux, Geoff Whitty, and Michael Young. Mahatma Gandhi and Rabindranath Tagore were given only limited importance in spite of their significant contributions to educational theory and pedagogy. Krishnamurti, who built alternative educational institutions in India and several other parts of the world and who influenced people worldwide, was given the least attention among Indian educators for being "too abstract" and for "not addressing issues of social change." Both these arguments, as my book testifies, are ill-founded and only express a lack of serious engagement on the part of Indian educators with Krishnamurti's work. The indifference toward Krishnamurti's work became apparent on several instances. In one of the courses I was denied to review Krishnamurti's book for it might be too difficult for the BEd students to follow. I was also discouraged from writing a master thesis on Krishnamurti; instead, I was suggested to write a thesis on Henry Giroux's philosophy of education. During this period, I questioned almost everywhere and everybody why Krishnamurti is absent from educational discourse in India, with no satisfactory answer in return. Nevertheless, I found references to Krishnamurti's work in the writings of Professor Krishna Kumar (2007), an introductory text by Vyas (1989) on Krishnamurti's educational ideas, and an excellent ethnographic study of Krishnamurti's Rishi Valley School in India by a renowned sociologist, Meenakshi Thapan ([1991] 2006).

Significantly, while I also became interested in the core principle of critical pedagogy—critical consciousness—I began to argue, because of my studies of Krishnamurti's work, that change in social structures is not enough. Consequently, I attempted to bring together Krishnamurti (an advocate of self-transformation) and Freire and Giroux (the proponents of social transformation) in my master's thesis. I wrote,

> It is significant to point out that the ideas of Krishnamurti and those of Freire and Giroux are different but not contradictory; rather, they are complimentary. For the latter, what is significant is the development of critical consciousness to understand and change oppressive social reality, while for Krishnamurti what is more significant is the understanding of how we, as individuals, play a role in bringing about and furthering the conflicts and problems of society. Both perspectives are essential and need to be combined for a true education that aims at a just, peaceful, and democratic society. (A. Kumar 2007, 10)

Thus, until 2007 I thought that Marxist and neo-Marxist thinking and what I learnt from Krishnamurti were totally reconcilable. My supervisor, Professor Shyam Menon[22], who did his postdoctoral work with Michael Apple at the UWM, agreed with me that it was important to look at social and personal change as related rather than as separate processes.

With this thinking I arrived at The University of British Columbia (UBC) in September 2007 to further explore the possibilities of integrating Krishnamurti's work with critical pedagogy and to develop a vision of social education that aims at personal and social transformation. In a paper—"Place of Critical Self-Awareness in a Social Education for Revolution"—that I presented at Rouge Forum conference in March 2008 at Louisville, I argued,

> Critical self-awareness can lay the foundation for actual psychological revolution that, in turn, can bring about change in the outer world as the latter has come into existence by each one of us through our thoughts and actions. Not that the structural changes are not essential but to focus only on them without focusing on their genesis and perpetuation in and through us is not going to bring about any substantial or fundamental change. Thus, change in one's consciousness is the real foundation for actual visible changes in the structure of the society. (A. Kumar 2008a)

I was surprised to find that at the Rouge Forum (a group of Marxist and neo-Marxist education scholars and activists), I was able to convey, though not without challenge, what I wanted, and the audience, though did not completely agree with me, found it difficult to undermine the importance of a fundamental self-transformation for any substantial social transformation to take place. While I continued to think that critical pedagogy and Krishnamurti could be successfully brought together, the above passage suggests that I, actually, began to articulate in its rudimentary form what I have discussed elaborately in this book. *That is, any fundamental change in social structures can only happen via transformation of our conflict-ridden consciousness, which, in actuality, lies at the base of wider structural problems.*

Fortunately, I had the opportunity to have email communication with Dr. Rich Gibson of San Diego State University, the best Marxist scholar I have met so far, on my Rouge Forum paper. This interaction further pushed my understanding regarding the differences between Marxism and the views of Krishnamurti. The more I thought the more disenchanted I became with my idea that I could bring critical pedagogy and Krishnamurti together; for, on the surface they seem to have agreement on the need for revolution and change, but at depth their ways to approach human conflicts are altogether different. Critical pedagogy, deriving its rationales in Marxist and neo-Marxist theories, is structure oriented; Krishnamurti's work, on the contrary, is consciousness oriented, and his vision of consciousness encompasses structures within it. My interactions with Professor William Pinar[23] on this paper and afterward further encouraged me to think on the importance of self-understanding.

Although I was doing fine in my course work, during the second year of my doctoral program I began to experience an inner intellectual crisis. I would often say to myself: Everybody is so much concerned with thinking and analysis, but why is nobody seeing that the very instrument—intellect—that we depend upon is an intrinsic part of our consciousness, which, as I can see, is in perpetual crisis. But, I was not sure what and how to say what was going on inside me. In the beginning, I used to speak a lot in classroom discussions, but slowly even the desire to say anything disappeared. I distinctly remember Professor Pinar asking me after a few classes in his course on autobiography: Why do you not speak in class? I tried to explain, but I knew that I could not possibly fully articulate what it is that was holding me back.

A major breakthrough for my doctoral research came when I got the opportunity to discuss *The Future of Humanity* (1986)—a small but dense book comprising of dialogues between Krishnamurti and David Bohm—in a doctoral seminar in Curriculum and Pedagogy with Professor Anne Phelan—who I deeply admired for her pedagogic approach that animated attentive and empathetic listening, criticality, and dialogue—in fall 2008. As I experienced it, seminar participants gave their minds and hearts to understand the content of the dialogues. It was the first formal occasion when I discussed Krishnamurti's work exclusively. It was a wonderful experience for we all engaged with passion. Not everybody agreed totally with Krishnamurti—and I did not expect the agreement at all—but Krishnamurti certainly left an impact for he was to be referred to quite often right through the course duration by my classmates. It was a transformative experience for me. It gave me tremendous confidence about my own thinking and search. For the first time, I began to feel that the inner work has to come out and be one with my intellectual work. No more was I ready to tolerate a split personality within me! It was after this class that I seriously began to think about conducting research regarding the educational significance of Krishnamurti's work.

Meanwhile, I was also getting feedback from my colleagues in the department that Professor Karen Meyer is interested in Krishnamurti's work and about her graduate level course, Living

Inquiry. However, I did not meet her personally until I decided to reorganize my doctoral committee.[24] The most important turning point for this research came when Professor Pinar remarked in a panel on Neoliberalism, Anti-intellectualism, and the Promise of the University: A Conversation, organized in 2009 by the Centre for Cross Faculty Inquiry at UBC: *If you pursue a research which you do not want to or are not interested in, you are perpetuating anti-intellectualism.* I would add that if you pursue a research which you are not interested in you are also sowing the seeds of mediocrity, dissatisfaction, and inward conflict within yourself.

The discontentment turned into the most significant initiative of my intellectual life when I decided to work on Krishnamurti as part of my doctoral dissertation and, fortunately, I got the best support—both intellectual and humanistic—a doctoral student can get. I asked for and I was given the *complete and unconditional freedom* to write on Krishnamurti[25] *the way I wanted* as part of my comprehensive examination papers. Those three comprehensive examination papers—"On the Nature of Consciousness," "On the Nature of Self-Inquiry," and "On the Nature of Education"—as well as an unpublished essay I authored regarding the important work of James Macdonald (A. Kumar, forthcoming), who has also influenced my thinking in the recent past, became the foundation for my doctoral research and the present book. My research and a really engaging and fruitful "complicated conversation" it provoked have brought into existence what I have decided to call *curriculum as meditative inquiry.*

Curriculum as meditative inquiry is a vision of education that is based on a deeper realization of the four key principles:

Human consciousness is in conflict.

Educational institutions reflect and perpetuate the characteristic features of human consciousness.

Meditative inquiry is an existential approach to comprehend and transform human consciousness.

Curriculum as meditative inquiry is a way to provide self-transformative educational experiences to students and their teachers.

The first principle—human consciousness is in conflict—explains that human consciousness, which is the basis of our thinking, feeling, and action, is common to all humanity and is in crisis. In other words, in spite of our cultural and personality differences deep down human consciousness is characterized by fear, conditioning, becoming, and fragmentation, which are common to all of us. Furthermore, our social, political, economic, and educational problems are not independent of but deeply connected to the nature of our consciousness. And since the features of our consciousness—for example, conditioning influences—and our social conflicts—for example, racial and nationalistic divisions—are deeply connected to one another, they cannot and should not be studied separately.

The second principle—educational institutions reflect and perpetuate the characteristic features of human consciousness—sheds light upon the interpenetrative relationship of consciousness and education. Contemporary educational institutions, being part and parcel of human consciousness, are affected by and affect the latter. They create in children a fear of authority, exams, and punishment. They also condition their minds with state-controlled and market-driven knowledge. In addition, modern educational institutions alienate children from their bodies, emotions, and spirits due to their overemphasis on cognitive learning. Since the nature of human consciousness and educational institutions are mutually connected and influence each other, we cannot and should not isolate problems of education, for example, discipline, from that of the larger consciousness, for example, fear.

The third principle—meditative inquiry is an existential approach to comprehend and transform human consciousness—underscores why meditative inquiry stands as a unique and viable approach to addressing conflicts of our consciousness. Since human consciousness is an existential phenomenon, is constantly changing, and is in flux, it cannot be understood and transformed entirely on the basis of theoretical, intellectual, or philosophical approaches. The latter use thinking, analysis, system, and authority as their foundations, which are based on thought, which in turn is based on memory and hence past. Thought, which is past, is unable to meet existential problems, for example, fear, that are always in the present. Meditative inquiry, which is to be aware of the movement of consciousness without analysis or judgment, is an existential approach to understanding and transforming consciousness. On the one hand, meditative inquiry underscores the limitations of thinking and analysis and, on the other hand, it emphasizes meditative listening and observation.

The final principle—curriculum as meditative inquiry is a way to provide self-transformative educational experiences to students and their teachers—is based on two perceptions: first, there is a close relationship between the nature of human consciousness and educational institutions; and second, meditative inquiry is a viable approach to understand and transform the human consciousness. Curriculum as meditative inquiry is a transformative approach to educational experience that aspires to undermine and possibly dissolve the conflicted nature of our consciousness by cultivating a deeper sense of awareness. Specifically, curriculum as meditative inquiry emphasizes the significance of arts of listening and seeing in educational process to have a deeper perception into one's own consciousness and one's relationships. It encourages the cultivation of the qualities of openness, aesthetics, and freedom in educational experience. Viewed from the perspective of meditative inquiry, education no more remains a problem of information transmission or means-end learning. On the contrary, it emerges as a space of freedom where the main focus is to learn about oneself and one's relationships to people, nature, and ideas.

In the next four chapters, I discuss each of these principles in detail.

CHAPTER 2

ON THE NATURE OF CONSCIOUSNESS

INTRODUCTION

Our home, planet earth, the only habitable and perhaps the most beautiful place in the entire universe, is in peril. An excellent documentary, *Home* (Arthus-Bertrand 2009), featured in the Vancouver Film Festival, explicitly shows the degenerating impact of human cultural evolution on the fragile ecosystem. Our earth, nevertheless, is not in danger because of ecological crisis only; the crisis is much deeper. In the process of cultural evolution, human beings have also achieved several other "distinctions" capable of destroying the earth. We have divided the *whole* earth into various nationalistic divisions, which have been, more often than not, in conflict with one another or preparing for the same by building their "defense." We have also divided ourselves by means of antagonistic religious, ideological, economic, and racial divisions. In short, we have produced a considerable crisis on the face of the earth especially in the past few hundred years endangering not only the existence of human beings but also that of the entire planet.

In the academic world there are several explanations for such a widespread crisis. For my purpose, I briefly discuss two major explanations: Marxist and psychoanalytic. From a Marxian perspective, the root of the majority of human problems is in the exploitative capitalist system. The Marxist solution to the human problems is rather straightforward: destroy capitalism and establish the rule of "proletariats," and then there will be equality, justice, and peace. In practice, such a disposition is antidemocratic, as it has been revealed by the state capitalism of erstwhile USSR and present-day China and Cuba.[1] In theory, the Marxist disposition is simplistic for it undermines human psychology and its impact on structures. In a Marxist conception, consciousness is an epiphenomenon; that is, consciousness is the product of structures.[2] I argue the contrary: *structures are basically crystallized forms of human consciousness.*[3]

That is, *there is only consciousness: consciousness as flux is thought or self; consciousness in crystallized form is structure.*[4] In other words, structures are not independent of human consciousness, and their formation, continuance, and destruction directly or indirectly is profoundly connected to human thought processes. So structures, for example, schools, more than representing themselves stand for those—human beings—who created them. Thus, I think it is critically significant that we give our serious consideration to understanding structures not only in their gross forms (e.g., capitalist system) but also in their subtle forms (e.g., accumulative psychology). In other words, *we must give close attention to the study of consciousness in its subtle (thought) as well as gross (structures) forms.*

From a psychoanalytic perspective, the major reason behind individual and social conflicts is not social and economic structures but consciousness itself, which is in perpetual conflict due to contradictions in its various layers: conscious and unconscious. Psychoanalysis is, I think, closer to human reality than Marxism. Its focus is on human beings—their actions, thoughts, and emotions—who actually create structures through their interactions. And, since human beings are in contradiction within themselves, they will naturally create contradictions and conflicts outside. Psychoanalysis however does not posit that human psychological conflicts can ever be resolved once and for all. At the most, human beings can become more aware of their psychological nature and modify themselves to live in relatively less conflict, inwardly and outwardly. What are we left with? The mind and society remain in conflict.[5]

In this chapter, I propose a third perspective on the nature of individual and social conflicts based on the works of Krishnamurti. In Krishnamurti's (1983, 9) perception,

> We are facing a tremendous crisis; a crisis which the politicians can never solve because they are programmed to think in a particular

way—nor can the scientists understand or solve the crisis; nor yet the business world, the world of money. The turning point, the perceptive decision, the challenge, is not in politics, in religion, in the scientific world; it is in our consciousness. One has to understand the consciousness of mankind, which has brought us to this point.

That is, *the real crisis is not in the systems but in the consciousness of human beings,*[6] *and the way out of this imminent crisis is in bringing about a radical transformation of the human psyche or consciousness through a deeper, meditative inquiry and understanding.* In this chapter, I will discuss the nature of consciousness and its conflicts. In the next chapter, I will discuss how characteristic features of larger consciousness influence the nature of contemporary educational institutions.

NATURE OF HUMAN CONSCIOUSNESS

In my understanding, the major reason behind why humanity on earth is in conflict—individually and socially (characterized by psychological strife, contradictions, anxiety and the problems of discrimination, inequality, wars, and environmental crisis)—lies in our consciousness or thought.[7]

The word consciousness means all the memories, experiences, beliefs, aspirations, symbols, and dogmas invented and put together by thought (Krishnamurti and Bohm 1986).[8] Human consciousness, which is the basis of thoughts, feelings, and actions, is common to all humanity. While there are cultural and personality differences, deep down human consciousness is characterized by psychological suffering, anxiety, pleasure, pain, conditioning, fear, fragmentation, and becoming (Krishnamurti 1983, 1991c; Krishnamurti and Bohm 1985, 1986). Considering Macdonald's (1966b) distinction between "individual" and "person" is also instructive here:

> The *person*, . . . in contrast to the individual, is not prized for his uniqueness. His uniqueness is simply a fact known to us through efforts of biological and psychological inquiry. The person is valued because of what he shares in common with all other persons: the human condition. Each person strives to create meaning of his existence in the world, and attempts to gain freedom from crippling fear, anxiety, and guilt. Each person shares the common fate of his morality and possesses the potential for expressing joy, awe, and wonder. The awareness

that all we know with certainty is that *we are here*, and that there are *others like us*, characterizes the human condition and makes the person of value. Thus, it is not the uniqueness of his personal perceptions, idiosyncratic needs, desires, and motives that make him of value; it is his common human status. (39–40)

In other words, in spite of our cultural and personality differences we all stand on the "same ground," for human consciousness or thought process functions more or less similarly. Take for example, the factor of fear, which is common to all of us. We all may have different kinds of fears and even ways to approach them, but fear exists as our psychological reality. Significantly, this emphasis that the consciousness of human beings is common has no totalizing intentions. The main reason behind such a view is, on the one hand, to discourage participation in the "crime of collectivism that identity politics commits" (Pinar 2009c, front page) and, on the other hand, to have this enormous perception that we all are part of, psychologically speaking, *one* humanity (Krishnamurti 1972). In my view, *thinking from the perspective of identity separates us from each other, whereas thinking from the perspective of consciousness brings us together*, because the latter helps us realize that we all, psychologically speaking, belong to each other. Now, I turn to discuss the factors of fear, conditioning, fragmentation, and becoming, which characterize human consciousness, with a particular consideration to what roles these factors play in the origination and continuation of individual and social conflicts.

FEAR AND INSECURITY

It seems reasonable to argue that fears are significant features of our beings, and our thoughts, feelings, and actions, directly or indirectly, are rooted in deep-seated fears. Krishnamurti considers fear among the central problems of human existence, as reflected by his enormous emphasis on understanding the nature and function of fear in almost all of his books.

What is fear and what causes it? Fear arises when we hold on to things or patterns (e.g., religious beliefs or political ideologies) that give us satisfaction; then, we are afraid of anyone or anything that may question deeply or take our attachments away from us. Krishnamurti elucidates (1969, 42),

I want to be reasonably certain of the state of things to which I am going. So the brain cells have created a pattern and those brain cells refuse to create another pattern which may be uncertain. The movement from certainty to uncertainty is what I call fear.

The origin of the inner conflicts is in the very process of holding on to beliefs to ward off psychological fear. Psychological accumulations, such as beliefs, prevent psychological fear as long as they are undisturbed. As medical knowledge helps to prevent physical pain, so do beliefs help to prevent psychological pain, and that is why most of us are afraid of losing our beliefs, though we might have no perfect knowledge or concrete proof of the reality of such beliefs (Krishnamurti 1954).

Psychological time is another significant factor behind fear. One might observe in oneself that thought (which is always old for being the response of memory) hardly rests in the present: it is either running into the future or dwelling upon the past. This constant movement where one wants either to reexperience pleasure or avoid pain also causes a sense of uncertainty and fear (Krishnamurti 1969).

Interestingly, "verbalization" at times can also function as a cause behind fear. For example, the very word death creates its own associated image(s) and thereby fears. "Am I afraid of the fact itself [for example, death]," Krishnamurti (1954, 188) asks, "or is that fear awakened because I have previous knowledge of the fact, knowledge being the word, the symbol, the image?" Certainly, word is not the thing; the word death is not death. But since mind thrives on words and the images it has formed, it creates fear even when in actuality there might be no reason for it (Krishnamurti 1969).

What are the implications of fear being a significant part of our beings? In *Transformation of Man*, Krishnamurti ([1979] 2005) discusses the question of fear, among other things, in great depth with David Bohm and David Shainberg, a theoretical physicist and a psychiatrist, respectively. Their discussions shed light upon how the prevalence of fear in the human psyche and social structures functions as the factor behind the search for psychological certainty and security through "acquisitiveness" and "self-aggrandizement." In my view, this seeking of psychological security to avoid dealing with the fact of fear has resulted in many personal and social problems. Consider, for example, the problems of accumulation, nationalistic and religious divisions, and discriminations.

In Marxian theory, *accumulation* is a structural—social, political, economic, and cultural—problem. While accumulation has undoubtedly resulted in deep economic inequalities between people, its actual roots are located in human psychology. Every human being, perhaps without exception, in one way or the other, is accumulating something—be it money, intellectual enhancement, or spiritual virtues—to feel secure and somehow escape fear (Krishnamurti and Bohm 1999). The psychological tendency to accumulate or what Macdonald ([1971b] 1995, 51) rightly calls the "ideology of achievement" has become the very soul of our social structure sustained by human psychology. Accumulative psychology also seems to me the cause behind the ever-expanding empire of capitalism, which certainly is based on the principles of pleasure, acquisitiveness, and self-aggrandizement. In Marxist conceptualization, capitalism is the result of technological advancement and unequal accumulation of capital. But, *is it possible to separate technology and unequal accumulation from human psychology?* In other words: *can we create anything that is independent of our psychological nature?* Following Macdonald's ([1974]1995, 75) theorization that technology is the externalization of the hidden consciousness of human potential, I would ask: Why did we create such a technology that brought about the capitalist system? Why has the capitalist system become global? Is it merely because of the capitalists who want to accumulate? Is not every human being interested in accumulation? Have not human beings always been interested in accumulation?

I think that what sustains capitalism is not the economic system alone but our accumulative psychology.[9] In other words, it is the general thought processes of human beings that support capitalism, which, in turn, strengthens and reinforces the former. Moreover, the emphasis on measurement and comparison (through standardized tests and grades in schools, publications and grants in academia, money and property in society, and the so-called heaven and hell in religious propaganda)—supported by positivism (epistemologically), capitalism (economically), and behaviorism (psychologically)—also stem from the nature of thought processes that are accumulative, comparative, and fragmentary. Put differently, *the psychological tendency to measure is in the root of materialism.*[10] John Dewey's (1930) remark that "quantification, mechanization, and standardization... have invaded mind and character, and subdued the soul to their own dye" (quoted in

Macdonald [1971b] 1995, 65) is deeply meaningful in this context. It is however important to make explicit that questioning the psychological tendency to accumulate does not mean to dispute any outward accumulation, such as the need of money to have a living or the training to learn a language; the real problem starts when we do things to seek psychological security.

Quite similar to the process of psychological accumulation is the issue of the *nationalistic divisions*: the ugliness that we have produced on the face of the earth by dividing it into various nation-states. Ironically enough, the idea that we are inhabitants of the earth or rather the universe looks abstract while being *real*, the idea of nationalistic divisions looks *real* in spite of being an ugly abstraction! It would be difficult for many of us to appreciate Krishnamurti's and my allegations regarding nationalistic divisions. Some of us might question: Is not a perspective that conceptualizes nationalistic divisions as bad and ugly reductionist? Is there nothing else associated with them, other ways of looking at nationalism that takes it out of just being ugly? Doesn't this ignore those nationalisms that attempt to blunt globalization, protect indigenous cultures, and respect human rights?

Historically speaking, nation-states have represented a tendency toward "glorified tribalism" (Krishnamurti 1984) responsible for mass murder in the name of seeking territories and resources. Such political divisions are not merely geographical but deeply psychological in nature where people herd together to feel secure.[11] Significantly, nationalism is only one of the many examples of how we have divided ourselves; there are numerous small nations within nations, cultures within cultures, and religions within religions. Considering the distinctions between geographical notions of *division* and *diversity* and between *spatial organization* and *psycho-spatial division* will be important to avoid a major conflation. Criticism of nationalistic divisions is not to question diversities in human landscape: different colors of skin, linguistic groups, food habits, dresses, literatures, and histories. My criticism of nationalism is primarily focused on those divisions that divide people along antagonistic lines. *It is entirely understandable to organize geographical space into manageable units, but what we see in the contemporary world is that lines are not only drawn on lands but also on the hearts and minds of people.* The chaos these territorial divisions have produced on the surface of the earth has been explicit throughout human history. Nationalism is certainly one of the major causes and effects of a fragmented and conflict-ridden humanity. Organized religions have served the same divisive function by playing upon fear, insecurity, and greed.

Discrimination—based on race, gender, and caste—is a major issue that modern academia shows its concern with, and rightly so. Although I have profound concerns for widespread discrimination, I think that the problem of discrimination is also a manifestation of conflicts in human relationships consequent upon the deep psychological fear of the "Other." And while there is no denial to the policy measures, such as antidiscrimination laws and structures, to take care of various forms of prejudices, I seriously think that the latter are highly inadequate to bring about any fundamental change. This is another major difference between Marxist theory and my understanding.

While for Marxist theory, changes in economic and political structures are a prerequisite and sufficient condition to bring about change in individuals and in creating a just society, in my view an emphasis on structures alone to bring about change in people and society is not only insufficient but also dangerous. Why? The belief that structures and laws alone can change human behavior reduces human beings to the status of machines, which can be programmed according to the "best" blueprint. The nature of human consciousness and the nature of relationships between human beings is a complex process that requires profound *understanding* rather than superficial treatments by means of laws and structures (Krishnamurti and Anderson 2000). *If individuals have understanding, their relationships (which is society) will be based on understanding rather than laws.*[12] Laws are important as guidelines but they cannot bring about deeper change of consciousness and compassion for the fellow human beings. On the contrary, over dependence on laws to define and maintain relationships signifies the prevalence of thoughtlessness.

Grounded in the understanding of the nature of human consciousness, and its conflicts, one is inclined to ponder whether the many forms of discriminations are merely social in origin and practice or are social manifestations of our psychological attitudes. Undoubtedly, one might trace as far back as possible in human evolution to find that the problem of discrimination has always existed not only between heterogeneous groups but also within homogenous groups. Casteism in India, which is thousands of years old, can serve as a very good example. The British were not the first to divide people in India; they accentuated already existing divisions for their own benefits.[13]

CONDITIONING INFLUENCES AND IMAGE-MAKING

Along with fear and insecurity deep-rooted *conditioning* of the human brain and the related process of *image-making* are also at the root of human conflicts. Contradicting Rousseau's (1954) claim that "[m]an is born free and everywhere he is in chains," Macdonald ([1971b] 1995, 53) argues,

> [M]an is born into chains and everywhere he tends to remain so. Man is chained at birth to his own internal needs and external conditions. He is neither free to survive in external environments, nor is he free to survive through the exercise of his internal structures.

What are these chains? *Conditioning influences.* The human brain, since the beginning of its evolution, has been subject to tremendous conditioning—biological and cultural. Whereas biological conditioning is a natural process, cultural conditioning by means of ideologies, religions, and education is dangerous because it divides people along antagonistic lines. Certainly, the profound sense of insecurity and fear and the preponderance of conditioning are bound together; insecure, uncertain, and fearful minds seek conditioning and allow it to take deep roots, while conditioning supports and sustains fear.

What is conditioning? Conditioning implies an incessant repetition of certain values, beliefs, and attitudes that shape the way people perceive the world. In Krishnamurti's (1970, 110) words,

> We are conditioned—physically, nervously, mentally—by the climate we live in and the food we eat, by the culture in which we live, by the whole of our social, religious and economic environment, by our experience, by education and by family pressures and influences. All these are the factors which condition us. Our conscious and unconscious responses to all the challenges of our environment—intellectual, emotional, outward and inward—all these are the action of conditioning. Language is conditioning; all thought is the action, the response of conditioning.

Moreover:

> En passant it is interesting to note that the so-called individual doesn't exist at all, for his [her] mind draws on the common reservoir of conditioning which he [she] shares with everybody else, so the division

between the community and the individual is false: there is only conditioning. This conditioning is action in all relationships—to things,
people and ideas. (111)

Crucially, it is the conditioning influences through which people
build *images* about themselves and others. And, it is due to these
images that there is no *real* relationship between people; all relationships are between psychological images. Since the image is the conclusion or abstraction of what one really is, there is constant conflict
between the "image" (which is abstract) and "actuality." It is due to
these images that we live "in ideas, in theories, in symbols...which
we have created about ourselves and others and which are not realities at all" (Krishnamurti 1969, 58–59). Consequently, all our relationships, whether they be with property, ideas or people, are based
essentially on this image-forming process, and hence there is always
conflict.

Moreover, it is for conditioning that we translate the present in
terms of past experience; under the influence of conditioning, if we
are unaware of it, we may even behave like a programmed computer.
Thus, conditioning influences of various sorts distorts our perceptions of reality. Evidently, an individual is not merely subject to a
homogenous set of conditioning; conditioning influences from different sources are more often than not in conflict with one another. For
example, one's religious conditioning may lead one to have faith in
God whereas one's scientific training may encourage one to doubt the
very existence of God. The different fragments of thought, produced
by different sources of conditioning influences, breed conflict and
cause the dissipation of energy.[14]

Furthermore, since different people have different conditioning
influences (e.g., ideological, religious, racial, cultural, economic, and
educational) they get in conflict with one another. Conditioning
influences thus have played a decisive role in dividing the entire world
among numerous fragments—racial, nationalistic, and religious. The
process of conditioning is certainly a key factor behind such widespread violence in the world. Krishnamurti (1969, 51) explains,

When you call yourself an Indian or a Muslim or a Christian or a
European, or anything else, you are being violent. Do you see why it is
violent? Because you are separating yourself from the rest of mankind.

When you separate yourself by belief, by nationality, by tradition, it breeds violence.

Significantly, it is the deep implications of psychological conditioning that society—parents, schools, organized religions, and political leaders—begin to shape consciously or unconsciously children's mind with their "best" values right in childhood. And one may see within one's own self how strong the impact of conditioning is the way one thinks, feels, and behaves in everyday situations.

Because of the apparent negative implications of the conditioning influences individually and socially, Krishnamurti (1969, 121) raises a significant question for us to ponder upon:

> [I]s it possible to break through this heavy conditioning of centuries immediately and not enter into another conditioning—to be free, so that the mind can be altogether new, sensitive, alive, aware, intense, capable?

In approaching conditioning influences the most significant thing to understand is that we should never look at them with justification or condemnation; then, we are not actually looking and learning but simply justifying, suppressing, or projecting. What is important is to be *aware* of our own selves in relationship to people, ideas, and nature. Relationship is like a "mirror" that reflects one's true self, if one is attentive. It is in relationships that one discovers whether one is mechanical, rigid, and repetitive or spontaneous, pliable, and creative (Krishnamurti 1992). Such self-discovery in relationships depends on the way one observes oneself in action, which forms relationships. Contrary to the commonly suggested ways to approach conditioning, Krishnamurti emphasizes the "total negation" of the past (including social morality, inward authority, pleasures, fulfillment, ideas, principles, and theories), psychologically speaking, through heightened awareness of one's thoughts, actions, and emotions. "Such negation," Krishnamurti (1970, 114) professes, "is the most positive action, therefore it is freedom."[15]

BECOMING AND PSYCHOLOGICAL TIME

Becoming is yet another factor behind psychological conflicts. Becoming is a psychological process of moving from "what is" to "what should be," which involves psychological time (Krishnamurti and Bohm 1985, 1986, 1999). Outwardly and structurally, there is no problem in moving away from "what is" to "what should be." For example, the intention of converting a barren land into a garden is a valid process that involves thinking and physical or chronological time. However, when it comes to a psychological movement involving psychological time to solve a psychological problem, for example, from fear to non-fear, the movement from "what is" to "what should be" proves destructive. Why? Because *the observer is the observed: The part of the thought that is fearful or angry (observed) and the part of the thought that wants to become fearless or non-angry (observer) are basically two aspects of one's thought.*[16] Becoming, therefore, is a separative process of thought that produces the illusion that the "observer" is different from the "observed" or the "thinker" is different from the "thought."[17] In actuality, it is only thought without any thinker. Readers may ask two questions here: Is it realistically possible to identify different "parts" of thought? And how can thought exist without a thinker?

In the preceding example of "fear to non-fear" I have identified a state of mind that we may not find ourselves in every moment. The states of strong emotions, such as fear or anger (where the distinction of the "observer" or "controller" and the "observed" or "controlled" is explicit), are not constant, generally speaking. But when they do appear, one can see the effort (suppression or indulgence) that one makes. So it is in strong emotions that we come to see conflict or contradiction in different parts of our beings. While usually it is only possible to see the division in a state of conflict, with increased awareness of one's thought processes one can see various fragments or what the Russian mystic, George Gurdjieff, calls "multiple 'I's" in our daily states of mind.[18]

Moreover, if one observes closely the movement of thought one comes to know that basically there is only thought without any thinker. The comprehension of the process of psychological fragmentation could help us understand this better. Thought is not a unitary movement; it is highly fragmented, and therefore there is contradiction and conflict. We feel the presence of the "thinker" because different fragments assume authority and create division between the "controller or observer" and the "controlled or observed." Interestingly, there is no permanent thinker or "I" as it generally appears to us. What we take to be a continual self is our abstraction based on memory, which also remains in flux. This abstraction in the form of a thinker may also be linked to the mind's search for security. Considering oneself a thinker or having an identity, which in reality is in constant flux, gives us a sense of continuity. What is the function of continuity? It is this sense of continuity or a search for security that there exists a "thinker" isolating itself constantly from the movement of "thought," and in the process creating a division within itself.

What is the outcome of the separative process between "the observer and the observed"? When thought separates itself as the "observer and the observed," there is a "controller" (e.g., the ideal of nonviolence) and the "controlled" (e.g., the fact of violence), which inevitably leads to suppression and conflict and in turn a waste of energy. Moreover, when we look at ourselves with an ideal in mind we have already gone against ourselves. Krishnamurti (1969, 48) elaborates,

> Some of us, in order to rid ourselves of violence, have used a concept, an ideal, called non-violence, and we think by having an ideal of the opposite to violence, non-violence, we can get rid of the fact, the actual—but we cannot. We have had ideals without number, all the sacred books are full of them, yet we are still violent—so why not deal with violence itself and forget the word altogether?[19]

Because of this divisive activity of the thought and the resultant conflict, "becoming" could be approached by "understanding," which is to be *aware* of the fact of fear or violence. It is important for us to realize that unless we have a perception—not an intellectual conclusion, but perceptive insight in our everyday lives and the divisions we create within ourselves—there is no possibility of resolving our psychological conflicts. We need to look at a fact without the screen of our prejudices, beliefs, opinions, and theories, which naturally form our conditioning. Since we have not learnt to look at things as they are, there are innumerable belief systems fighting against one another to prove which way of looking at problems is the best. Basically, we should ask ourselves if it is possible to look within our selves and our relationships with people, things, and ideas without images, opinions, and interpretations. In other words: Can we live with "that which is" or the "facts" without distorting them?

One may ask: What would it mean not to "distort" what one comes across? Doesn't that imply an "objectivist" perspective, for example, a non-perspectival perspective? Is not the viewer always part of what is viewed? Usually, when we look at something or listen to somebody or something there is the barrier of knowledge—what one already knows—between oneself and phenomena. Observation or listening from preestablished knowledge is a state of non-awareness or non-meditativeness. If the human capacity to know was limited by memory, conditioning or past, then there was no possibility for creative insights and inventions. Creative insights happen when the mind is silent. A silent mind—that is not projecting itself on what it encounters—does not distort reality. It comes into contact with things as they are and that is why it sees what is generally overlooked or distorted. In this sense, the viewer becomes one with viewed in an existential way, but not in the sense of overshadowing the viewed.

FRAGMENTATION AND CONFLICT

Fragmentation connotes a state of affairs where different parts—within an individual and in society—are in mutual discord, which inevitably leads to conflict and degeneration.[20] The preceding discussion can very well be understood as an explication of the widespread social and psychological fragmentation and resultant conflict. Fear, as I discussed above, is a tremendous factor of fragmentation in individuals and society. It is due to fear and a deep sense of insecurity, which brings about accumulation, nationalistic and religious divisions, and discriminations of all sorts, that there exists widespread fragmentation.[21] Conditioning influences and image-making, which are also discussed above, fuel fragmentation and conflicts within and between individuals and groups. Finally, the process of psychological becoming or time, also discussed above, is another form of fragmentation between the "ideal and actual" and the "thinker and thought," leading to psychological conflict and a waste of energy. In this section I will discuss the issue of fragmentation in more detail in light of David Bohm's[22] *Wholeness and the Implicate Order*[23] in particular and Krishnamurti's works in general.

The growth and development of human civilization has happened in a rather fragmentary way, which has brought about diverse, and more often than not, antagonistic nationalistic, religious, political, economic, and racial groups.[24] We have also viewed nature as an aggregate of separately existent parts, to be conquered and exploited by different groups of people. Besides, each individual human being has also been subject to psychological fragmentation and conflict due to conditioning influences of various sorts, as I noted above, "to such an extent that it is generally accepted that some degree of neurosis is inevitable, while many individuals going beyond the 'normal' limits of fragmentation are classified as paranoid, schizoid, and psychotic etc." (Bohm 1980, 2).

Such widespread and pervasive divisions between people (racial, nationalistic, religious, and ideological) and within each individual, which prevent us from being at peace within ourselves and from bringing about peace and harmony in our relationships with other people, have been brought about by the thought processes that treat things as "inherently divided, disconnected, and 'broken up'" (Bohm 1980, xii). Under the influence of divisive, fragmentary, and isolated thinking, people tend to defend their needs against others and the need of the group they identify with against other groups as primary, rather than thinking of the need of the whole of humanity. Such a worldview, which considers people and their world as fragmented is a kind of illusion because the whole universe is undivided, has brought us to ecological crisis, wars, and worldwide political and economic disorder.

Additionally, the fragmentation has also been widespread as a consequence of an almost "universal habit of taking the content of our thought for 'a description of the world as it is'" (Bohm 1980, 4). In other words, our thought is regarded as in direct contact with objective reality. However, in view of the understanding that our minds are deeply conditioned, what we see inside and outside is not reality but our projection on reality. Since our thinking is governed by fragmentary thoughts, whatever we throw our eyes on becomes fragmented.

Another major source of fragmentation is the generally accepted notion that the process of thinking is sufficiently independent of its content, which allows us to carry out clear, orderly, rational thinking, capable of judging the content as correct or incorrect, rational or irrational, fragmentary or whole. But, the actuality is totally opposite: fragmentation is characteristic of both the process of thinking as well as its content (Bohm 1980, 23). In fact, content and process are not separately existent things, but, rather, they are two aspects of the one whole movement, very much like "thinker and thought" are the two aspects of the same movement.

In their response to the widespread fragmentation, Krishnamurti and Bohm do not propose any imposed integration of thought or societal fragments; for, such an imposed integration will be another fragment. Notably, the Marxist emphasis on class consciousness and the unity of the proletariat is nothing but a process of bringing about further fragmentation and conflict. Similarly, the psychological emphasis on bringing together the disparate parts of one's consciousness is not feasible as long as the "I," or the "observer" (an abstracted entity from the "stream of consciousness or thought") is separated from the "observed" through psychological time.

For the sake of clarity and to avoid a conflation, I must make it clear here that measurement, analysis, and division to separate things to reduce them to manageable proportions in our practical-technical world is essential, for it is impossible to take care of the whole universe together. Likewise, our awareness of being separate from nature is very useful in developing autonomy in our thinking and going beyond nature's limits. But, the fragmentary worldview becomes destructive and negative when we look at ourselves, our relationships to people and nature and the whole world as separate, isolated, and self-existent units (Bohm 1980).

Moreover, different ways of thinking are simply different ways of looking at the reality, and each way can be appropriate in a particular domain. Thus, one way of thinking should not be blindly employed to understand other domains. (The application of positivism to understand human issues, such as education, can be considered as an example here.) Hence, the application of measurement, analysis, and classification have a meaning in technical, functional, and practical works, but the former result in fragmentation when we extend their application beyond their appropriate domain (Krishnamurti and Bohm 1999), which in effect is "an attempt to divide what is really indivisible" (Bohm 1980, 20).

The next error begins when we "try to unite what is not really unitable" (Bohm 1980, 20) such as the formation of various social, political, and economic groupings. As I pointed previously, nations and religious organization are based on the *principle of identification* with a larger unit to escape physical and psychological fear and insecurity.[25] By their very nature such groups tend to be in conflict with one another. Moreover, each individual also sees himself or herself as a separate fragment ("I" or Ego) and thus is in conflict with rest of the people in the same group. Even worse, each individual is the result of numerous fragments, which are also in conflict. Fragmentary viewpoint breeds conflict within and between individuals and groups. According to Bohm (1980, 20), "True unity in the individual and between man [human beings] and nature, as well as between man and man [human beings], can arise only in a form of action that does not attempt to fragment the whole of reality."

In essence, fragmentation basically represents serious confusions around the question of difference and sameness, and "*to be confused about what is different and what is not, is to be confused about everything*" (Bohm 1980, 21; emphasis in original). The distinction that I made previously between division and diversity and spatial organization and psycho-spatial division may be recalled here. Certainly, I am not for a totalitarian uniformity; however, dividing human beings, geographically and otherwise, is surely akin to a "murderous act" (Herbertson [1915] 1996).[26] It is obviously the wrong application of the notion of "difference" that is leading to such a widespread range of crisis in every sphere of human life.

Undoubtedly, it is important and urgent that we focus our energies to understand the nature and implications of fragmentation that penetrates the whole of our lives. "What is the use of attempts at social, political, and economic or other action," Bohm (1980, 21) asks, "if the mind is caught up in a confused movement in which it is generally differentiating what is not different and identifying what is not identical?" The critical question for us is: How are we to think coherently of a single, unbroken, flowing actuality of existence as a whole, containing both thought (consciousness) and external reality as we experience it (Bohm 1980)? Even beyond: How shall we realize in the very core of our beings that life exists in relationships, and any isolating act, individually or socially, will bring about fragmentation, conflict, and the dissipation of energy?

First, we must realize, as the notion of "undivided wholeness" (Bohm 1980) portends, that consciousness or thought and the reality are not two separate substances but different aspects of one whole and unbroken movement. Second, the ending of the fragmentation requires perspicacious meditation or awareness—a really arduous process—to the whole movement of thought. And the intensity of the attention depends on our level of realization that we have been living, psychologically and socially, with the fragmentary thought processes, which have, as I have dealt above, resulted in widespread global disorder. In chapter 4, I will discuss about the nature of meditative inquiry that may help us to have deeper insights into the nature of our conflict-ridden consciousness.

CONCLUSION

The innumerable problems with which our earth is plagued—be it nationalistic, ideological, racial or religious conflicts, discrimination and exploitation, or ecological crisis—are due to the conflict in human consciousness, human relationships, and humankind's relationship with nature. Consciousness is a vast realm that also encompasses our structures, for the latter are deeply connected to the former, or rather more precisely structures are externalized forms of our psychological nature. It is therefore important for us to understand the nature of our consciousness and the ways in which our consciousness takes shape in different forms and dimensions, including the domain of education. In other words, we must realize that there cannot exist anything in our society, which in one way or another is not related, explicitly or implicitly, directly or indirectly, to our psychological nature. Thus, we need to give our energy to understanding *the psychological structure of the society*. That is, rather than merely taking care of the flowers and leaves, which are the structures of society, we need to move deeper, into the roots, into our consciousness, which through thoughts, feelings, and actions creates society.

Notwithstanding the critical significance of the nature of human consciousness, academic discourses place enormous emphasis on structures (Marxism and its various off shoots) and text (postmodernism). Even those theoretical stances—phenomenology, existentialism, and psychoanalysis—that emphasize subjectivity or subjective consciousness also limit human subjectivity to human experiences and memories. That is to say, consciousness is either seen as an epiphenomenon (Marxism and neo-Marxism), discourse (postmodernism), or assemblages of complex human experiences and aspirations (phenomenology-psychoanalysis-existentialism). Krishnamurti, on the other hand, points toward something deeper in our beings which is "untouched and uncontaminated" by thought (beliefs, conditioning influences, memories, experiences, emotions, and aspirations). It is this dimension that Krishnamurti calls "awareness"—beyond the limits of thought in each one of us and outside—that materialist thinking has avoided dealing with.[27] I think it is toward the free "space" in ourselves that Krishnamurti is pointing attention, which he thinks will not be perceived if we try to suppress or rationalize or theorize "self" or "thought." What is important for us is to watch ourselves without any judgment, condemnation, or appreciation. Underscoring the importance of this very watchfulness, witnessing or awareness, which may reveal the content of thought, is one of the central concerns of curriculum as meditative inquiry. It is this state of mind where thought has come to a silence or consciousness is in order—not contrived or forced but through meditative understanding of its own movement—that has the potential of bringing order to the everlasting conflict within and between people.[28] In the next chapter I will discuss how the characteristic features of consciousness—fear, conditioning, becoming, and fragmentation—reflect themselves in the domain of education.

Chapter 3

On the Nature of Education

Introduction

Contemporary educational institutions are greatly affected by and in turn affect and perpetuate the conflict-ridden nature of human consciousness. "[S]chools...," Macdonald ([1971b] 1995, 51) argues, "are a living embodiment of the very shoddiness that pervades our general social [and psychological] experience...a rather faithful replica of the whole." Schools represent, Macdonald (1975a, 4) thinks, "a microscopic paradigm of a macroscopic human condition, a paradigm that holds all of the complexities in microcosm of the larger condition." Contemporary educational institutions, being part of the larger consciousness, in most cases, contribute to making students as well as teachers fearful of the authority of nation-states, the market, society, and exams. They also condition children's minds with dominant sociocultural practices, political ideologies, and market (and in some cases religious) propaganda thereby distorting their perceptions as well as dividing human beings along racial, religious, ideological, and nationalistic lines. Modern educational institutions also hinder a meditative state of mind by constantly pushing children to become "somebody important" through pursuing ambitions and big ideals instead of encouraging them to learn deeply about their own selves. Finally, contemporary educational institutions bring about fragmented personalities due to their overemphasis on children's intellect or cognition at the expense of the physical, emotional, and spiritual aspects of their beings.[1]

In this chapter I discuss how the characteristic features of con-sciousness—fear, conditioning, becoming, and fragmentation—shape and control the nature of our contemporary educational institutions as well as probe their potential effects on the growth and development of children.

FEAR: AUTHORITY, DISCIPLINE, AND CONFORMITY

We begin to acquire many *fears*—of darkness, strangers, and punishment—in our very childhood at home and in school. Evidently, our socialization at any level hardly plays a significant part in providing us with the opportunity to understand (not suppress or hide) our fears, which, as we grow up, dominate our attitudes and judgment and create several problems in different spheres of our lives. It is because of the significant role fear plays in our lives, Krishnamurti (1953, 35) thinks,

> The right kind of education must take into consideration this question
> of fear, because fear warps our whole outlook on life. To be without
> fear is the beginning of wisdom, and only the right kind of education
> can bring about the freedom from fear in which alone there is deep
> and creative intelligence.

In what ways do educational institutions cultivate fear? While there are many factors that cultivate fear among children, for the sake of brevity I discuss three most important of them, namely, authority, discipline, and conformity. The factor of *authority* in the psychologi-cal sphere plays a key role in cultivating fear among children. While talking to students and teachers in his school at Rajghat (India), Krishnamurti (1999b, 45) raises a crucial question: "Why is it that we accept authority?" Basically, acceptance of authority has its roots in fear. It is out of the fear of getting lost, rejection, and failure that we depend on others. Depending on others in the technical field is obvious, but there is great danger when we depend on somebody to tell us what is "right" in the psychological sphere. Psychological dependency and fear undermines the growth and development of our creative intelligence. "Acceptance of authority," Krishnamurti (1999b, 45) considers, "is a form of imitation... [, and] imitation begins only when you accept what another person says and... you imitate, because you are afraid to stand alone." Naturally, considering what parents, teachers, and leaders think is right gives a sense of security to children. "[U]nless you begin now—as you are growing up—to [question and] understand this extraordinary instinct to imitate, to accept, to obey," Krishnamurti (46) urges children, "you will find yourself functioning from day to day like a repetitive machine."[2]

To question authority, which is the beginning of intelligence, is troublesome for both elders and children. Children obviously depend on parents and teachers for their sustenance and education. Elders do not want to be questioned, perhaps, because they do not have time in this work-obsessed and success-driven world, or they do not consider discussing issues of fear and authority important, or maybe they do not think that they are able to engage children in such discussions, as their parents might never have encouraged them to question what or whom they depended on or were fearful of. Drawing upon his North American experience and observations, Macdonald ([1971a] 1995, 44) remarks,

> Teachers often avoid controversial issues, deny the erotic aspects of the nature of human beings, and avoid the discussion of anything which is not planned ahead of time. Many teachers are consumed by the fear that they will loose control, that some situation will present itself in which they must operate as a responsive human being rather than a status symbol of authority. Under these sorts of circumstances, it pays to get things "organized" and to develop managerial techniques whose primary goal is the maintenance of control.

I must clarify that encouraging children to question parents' and teachers' authority is not asking for a superficial rebellion that we generally see in children, especially in adolescents, to pursue their desires and pleasures without any consideration and care. Emphasis on discontentment and questioning is to be full of consideration and care for the elders, but without succumbing to their undue demands for conformity and obedience, because imitation, acceptance, and obedience bring about and strengthen fear. Thus, questioning should not only be directed from students to parents and teachers; it should be self-directed as well as mutual in the form of a dialogue, which may help them all—students, parents, and teachers—to go deeper into the issues. When conducted respectfully, such a dialogue may also bring them closer to one another in profound communication.

Discipline, like authority, has been a key factor in our social structure due to political, military, and industrial reasons. The notion of
discipline is also deeply psychological. "[I]t is because of our desire to
be psychologically secure," Krishnamurti (1953, 31) argues, "that we
accept and practice various forms of discipline. Discipline guarantees
a result, and to us the end is more important than the means; but the
means determine the end." In all social institutions including schools,
discipline instead of intelligence and sensitivity has played a significant role in controlling and organizing people.

Overemphasis on order and discipline via bureaucratic mentality
and hierarchical domination—as evident in "our reporting, grading, and testing practices, our authoritarian relationships, and our
prizing of docility, punctuality and attendance" (Macdonald [1971a]
1995, 41); "definition of roles and status, appropriate agencies, procedures of referral, proper procedures per se, and avenues of redress";
"[c]ategorization of students by ability, grade level, unit level etc. "
(Macdonald [1975c] 1995, 114); "the compulsion to have things run
smoothly, to be efficient, to be accountable for goals, and thus to
control the social behavior of students " (Macdonald [1975c] 1995,
123); and hierarchical or authoritarian determination of "the goals of
the teacher, subject syllabus...with whom they [students] will associate with in schools, where they will go at a given time, why they
are doing what they are, what they are doing, or when they will do
it" (Macdonald 1995, 150)—implies "autocratic" (Macdonald 1995,
150) and military-industrial orientation of our schools as well as lack
of our trust in worth, dignity, and integrity of individuals.[3]

Indeed, schools in many ways operate like "total institutions"
(Goffman 1961, xv) such as prisons and mental institutions, because
they have a formal set of prescriptions and proscriptions to control
inmate conduct, defined rewards in exchange for obedience, and
punishment against acts of violations (Macdonald [1971a] 1995, 43).
Thus, the responsibility of schools and teachers is unfortunately not
to be concerned with "'how students learn and develop'...but how to
construct effective and orderly activities within which students learn
and develop" (Macdonald [1975b] 1995, 114).

How can sensitivity, a sense of responsibility, and intelligence be
ever awakened through compulsion and lack of trust? Guided consciously or unconsciously by behaviorism, schools try to bring order
among children through controlling their outward behavior without

delving into the psychological realm where, in actuality, the problem first originates. Krishnamurti (1953, 32) elaborates,

> One may compel a child to be outwardly quiet, but one has not come face to face with that which is making him obstinate, impudent, and so on. Compulsion breeds antagonism and fear. Reward and punishment in any form only make the mind subservient and dull.

Discipline implies control, resistance, and conflict, and it can never lead to understanding and intelligence. "Implicit in right education," Krishnamurti (1953, 33) points out, "is the cultivation of freedom and intelligence, which is not possible if there is any form of compulsion, with its fears." The concern of the educator should be to help students understand the complexities of his or her whole being rather than compelling them to suppress one part of their personality for the benefit of some other part; for, suppression inevitably leads to inward and outward conflict. "[W]hen human beings are regimented in any way," Krishnamurti contends, "keen awareness and intelligence are destroyed" (34). "It is intelligence," Krishnamurti stresses, "that brings order, not discipline" (33).

The demand on the part of teachers and parents for *conformity* and obedience from children without having any respect for them also bring about fear. "When the showing of respect to elders is required of children," Krishnamurti (1953, 33–34) maintains, "it generally becomes a habit, a mere outward performance, and fear assumes the form of veneration." When teachers and parents demand respect from children without having any respect for them, the obvious consequence is the prevalence of indifference and disrespect among children for their elders. Moreover, there is no real respect for another when there is a reward for it, because the bribe or the punishment becomes far more significant than the inward feeling of respect. If we have no respect for the children but merely offer them a reward or threaten them with punishment, we are encouraging acquisitiveness and fear.

CONDITIONING INFLUENCES: NATIONALISM AND ORGANIZED RELIGION

It would not be unreasonable to argue that education, at home, in society, and in educational institutions, by and large, has been used as a means to propagate a mind-set that is in consonance with the existing system. If education remains limited to the level of transmission of the traditionally accepted notions, it simply serves as a means of perpetuating *conditioning*. Through conditioning, we "protect" our children and "shape their ways of thinking and feeling" by molding them into established patterns of society (Krishnamurti 1953, 28).[4] Thus, present-day educational institutions do not "encourage the understanding of the inherited tendencies and environmental influences which condition the mind and heart and sustain fear" (29).

What are the major factors that bring about deep psychological conditioning? As soon as the child is born he or she enters the realm of conditioning influences, all of which, of course, are not destructive in nature. We certainly need memory and thought to carry out our daily functions, to learn music and mathematics, as well as to develop language skills to communicate with one another. Nevertheless, there also exist conditioning influences—nationalism, racism, religious fundamentalism, and consumerism—that are inherently destructive in nature. Of particular interest are the conditioning influences from the nation-states and the organized religions.

Throughout history education has been used as a means to reinforce the "territorial imperative" (Ardrey 1997) among children. Even the great Indian epics such as *Mahabharata* and *Ramayana*, which are thousands of years old, clearly show the ancient human quest for territorial possessions. The territorial divisions and the conflicts they have produced in the modern world, as reflected through nationalism, imperialism, colonialism, and the resultant regional and World Wars, are well documented. It would not be an exaggeration to contend, as I also noted previously, that *nationalism* has functioned as a major factor in giving rise to a fragmented and conflicted human civilization. It also would not be an overstatement to argue that the modern nation-states have used education as one of its "ideological apparatuses" (Althusser 1971) to shape children's minds according to narrow nationalistic agendas. In addition to the general ethos of schooling, history and civics education have played crucial roles in cultivating nationalistic identities, which are more often than not in conflict with one another. In *Education as a Political Tool in Asia* (2009) Marie Lall and Edward Vickers, professors at the Institute of Education of the University of London, have collected invaluable case studies from nine Asian countries to depict how education is used as an ideological instrument to meet political ends (see also A. Kumar 2013).

Likewise, Krishna Kumar, an iconic contemporary Indian educator who is also influenced by Krishnamurti's perceptions, has shown through his studies—*Prejudice and Pride* (2001) and *Battle for Peace* (2007)—the vicious role nationalist propaganda play in shaping the perceptions of children in Indian and Pakistani schools.

Religious education at home and in schools has also been a major factor of destructive conditioning. Organized religions (their dogmas, rituals, mysteries, superstitions, sacred books, mediators, and ways of threatening and holding people) and their conditioning influences (by means of the so-called religious education) are responsible factors behind widespread hatred and violence among human beings. Those of us who are religiously inclined try to impose upon the child the beliefs, hopes, and fears, which they in turn have acquired from their parents; and those of us who are antireligious (e.g., Marxists with their "holy trinity" of Marx-Engels-Lenin and Bible, *Capital*) are equally keen to influence the child to accept the particular ways of thinking that they themselves happen to follow.

It is crucial to point out here that although Krishnamurti was extremely critical of the so-called religious education that perpetuates organized beliefs, he, actually, suggested that a right kind of education is essentially religious in nature (Forbes 1994). Significantly, Krishnamurti's emphasis on the religious education is diametrically opposite to its dogmatic forms. While dogmatic religious education cripples children's capacities to ask questions, Krishnamurti's view of religious education gives highest importance to questioning and doubt. In Krishnamurti's (1953, 39) view: "It is only when we inquire into the significance of the values which society and religion have placed about us that we begin to find out what is true." *True religious education is not a form of conditioning. Its purpose is to guide children on the path of self-inquiry and freedom, which brings virtue.* According to Krishnamurti (1953, 41),

> If those who are young have the spirit of inquiry, if they are constantly searching out the truth of all things, political and religious, personal and environmental, then youth will have great significance and there is hope for a better world.

Evidently, in spite of the destructive role of the conditioning influences, contemporary educational institutions do not appear to encourage children and teachers to understand their conditioning and how that conditioning operates in their interactions with fellow human beings. When educational institutions only serve the vested interests of society without providing opportunities for delving into the profound psychological conditioning of the educator and educated, they may produce well-programmed computers rather than individuals who have the potential for creative growth and transformation.[5] *Recognizing the lack of emphasis on self-understanding in educational institutions, I think that the primary function of education should be to provide opportunities for teachers and students to inquire into their psychological nature.* This inquiry into one's own conditioning, which influences one's whole being, is the beginning of intelligence and creativity. "There can be integrated action only," Krishnamurti maintains, "if one is aware of one's own conditioning, of one's racial, national, political and religious prejudices; that is, only if one realizes that *the ways of the self are ever separative*" (1953, 45; emphasis added).

Realizing the deleterious nature of conditioning influences, the right kind of educator appreciates the critical significance of "the inward nature of freedom" and helps children to "observe and understand" their "self-projected values and impositions" as well as "become aware of the conditioning influences" about them both of which limit their minds and breed fear (Krishnamurti 1953, 29). "Neither conformity to the present society nor the promise of a future Utopia," Krishnamurti maintains, "can ever give to the individual that insight without which he is constantly creating problems" (29). *Radical transformation is only possible when we understand our conditioning and be free of it.*

BECOMING: AMBITIONS AND IDEALS

Becoming in the context of education can be understood in terms of two constructs: ambition and ideal. What are we being educated for? Is it not to turn out, "as if through a mould, a type of human being whose chief interest is to find security, to become somebody important, or to have a good time with as little thought as possible (Krishnamurti 1953, 9)?" Krishnamurti (1953, 11) inquires further:

> [W]hat is the significance of life? What are we living and struggling for? If we are being educated merely to achieve distinction, to get a

better job, to be more efficient, to have wider domination over others, then our lives will be shallow and empty. If we are being educated only to be scientists, to be scholars wedded to books, or specialists addicted to knowledge, then we shall be contributing to the destruction and misery of the world.

Right from the beginning we implant a cancer of *ambition* or what Macdonald ([1971b] 1995, 51) calls an "ideology of achievement" instead of a love for learning in the innocent beings of children. Once ambition takes roots in the delicate minds of children, they enter this barbaric culture of capitalism, positivism, and behaviorism (or the culture of materialism, if put together), which is essentially based on the principles of reward and punishment, or more succinctly fear. Influenced consciously or unconsciously by the system of reward and punishment, "[s]tudents...," Macdonald ([1975c] 1995, 123) remarks, "work for grades, teachers approval, test results, parental approval, to competitively best other students. These rewards are not 'in the interest' of students in terms of the intrinsic value of activity in their everyday lives." Instead of drawing joy from working on the activities they like, students work hard to please others to get what Macdonald calls "socially abstracted pleasure" (124). As students spend more time in the reward oriented system and have internalized its principles, repression of creative behavior and alienation becomes unavoidable (124).

Unfortunately, the struggle for children to become something other than what they are begins at a time when they should start learning about themselves and their environment. This struggle born of ambitions brings about anxiety and fear and cripples intelligence. "Any form of ambition, spiritual or mundane," Krishnamurti (1964, 10) stresses, "breeds anxiety, fear; therefore ambition does not help to bring about a mind that is clear, simple, direct, and hence intelligent."

What is commonly emphasized in conventional educational institutions is not being different from the group or developing the ability to question and resist the environment. On the contrary, conventional educational institutions encourage children to be respectful of authority and tradition and worship success, which is the pursuit of reward. This whole ambition and success-driven approach to education "smothers discontent, puts an end to spontaneity and breeds fear; and fear blocks the intelligent understanding of life" (Krishnamurti 1953, 9–10). Conventional educational institutions, which primarily encourage conformity, thus make independent thinking extremely difficult and thereby breeds mediocrity. Krishnamurti (1953, 44) explains further:

> As long as success is our goal we cannot be rid of fear, for the desire to succeed inevitably breeds the fear of failure. That is why the young should not be taught to worship success. Most people seek success in one form or another, whether on the tennis court, in the business world, or in politics. We all want to be on top, and this desire creates constant conflict within ourselves and with our neighbors; it leads to competition, envy, animosity and finally to war.

Since society is the relationship between each one of us, and if our relationship is based on ambition, each one of us wanting to be more powerful than the other, then obviously our relationships (which is society) will always be in conflict. According to Krishnamurti (1964, 51), "The very pursuit of power—power for ourselves, power for our country, power for an ideology—is evil, destructive, because it inevitably creates opposing powers, and so there is always conflict." Moreover, "education based on individual advancement and profit," Krishnamurti (1953, 36) contends, "can only build a social structure which is competitive, antagonistic and ruthless."

Is there an alternative to ambition, competitiveness, pursuit of power, and the resultant conflict? "You will find the right answer," Krishnamurti suggests, "when you love what you are doing... [I]f you really love to be an engineer, or a scientist or if you can plant a tree, or paint a picture, or write a poem, not to gain recognition but just because you love to do it, then you will find that you never compete with another. *I think this is the real key: to love what you do*" (1964, 52–53; emphasis added). *Certainly, the real purpose of education should not be to cultivate the pursuits of success, ambition, and power within children, but help them find what they love and are passionate about.* And, naturally, if children love what they do they are more likely to give their whole being to it.

While primarily teaching students to be ambitious and successful we commit another violence with them, a violence of teaching them to pursue big *ideals*, the ideals of peace, truth, and nonviolence. What are ideals? Ideals in their simplest sense refer to something opposite to what actually exists. For example, the ideal of nonviolence is the opposite of the actuality of violence that has been within us and in our society. Educational ideals can be most destructive in nature as far as the development of creative self-understanding among teachers and students is concerned. Why?

First, when we educate children for ideals, which are inevitably future oriented, we shape them according to our conception of that future. The danger of enclosing children in the framework of an ideal is to encourage them to conform to the established pattern. Such conformity leads to fear, which in turn produces in children a constant conflict between "what they are" and "what they are expected to be." Individuals in conflict will obviously create a society in conflict as "all inward conflicts have their outward manifestations in society" (Krishnamurti 1953, 26). It is only by encouraging students to understand themselves as they are without imposing how they should be that there could be transformation that is not predetermined, predestined, and preconceived.

Second, following an ideal, pattern, or formula is equal to living a very superficial and mechanical life. Certainly, to live for an ideal or utopia demands sacrificing the understanding of the complexity of one's inner and outer circumstances. Human beings are not machines; they are "living beings who are impressionable, volatile, sensitive, afraid, affectionate" (Krishnamurti 1953, 27) and, thus, cannot be forced to follow a plan for utopia. *Life is change, movement, and flux; it cannot be made to conform to a system or framework, however nobly conceived.* The mind that is forced to follow a pattern becomes incapable of "thinking intelligently" and thus is "incapable of meeting life [as a whole] with its variety, its subtlety, its depths and great heights" (24). Krishnamurti raises some crucial questions for utopia-oriented dreamers:

[W]ho are we to decide what man [woman] should be? By what right do we seek to mould him [her] according to a particular pattern, learnt from some book or determined by our own ambitions, hopes and fears? (1953, 23)

The purpose of true education, Krishnamurti (1953, 23) thinks, is to help "the individual to be mature and free, to flower greatly in love and goodness. That is what we should be interested in, and not in shaping the child according to some idealistic pattern."

On the surface, it seems absolutely all right to respond to the deep-seated psychological and social problems (e.g., violence) by inventing ideals (e.g., the ideal of nonviolence). But, is it possible in actuality to solve our psychological and social problems by inventing ideals? We have had ideals of peace and nonviolence for thousands of years but so far we have only experienced ever-growing violence in its ugly and brutal forms. Evidently, by emphasizing these ideals rather than encouraging children to understand the actual states of their own minds and the society, we have brought about inner conflict and outward hypocrisy. Is Krishnamurti pro-violence? Of course not. Krishnamurti is against pursuing the *ideal* of nonviolence. Krishnamurti has a *negative approach* to deal with violence, which is to understand and go deeper into conflict and violence to know its psychological source and mechanism. Through the negation of the actual—violence—may come the flower of nonviolence within individuals and society at large. I will discuss the meaning and significance of the negative approach in next chapter.

FRAGMENTATION: PSYCHOLOGICAL, NEUROLOGICAL, SPIRITUAL, AND SOCIAL

In what ways do our contemporary educational institutions contribute toward fragmentation within individuals and society? First, when educational institutions impose authority and discipline and encourage conformity, they cultivate fear. Certainly fear is responsible for suppressing those dimensions of children's beings that are not in consonance with respected norms. This suppression results in the conflict or fragmentation within children as well as between children and their parents and teachers. Second, in most cases educational institutions encourage "becoming" through emphasizing ambitions and ideals. More often than not children are, consciously or unconsciously, discouraged to learn what they really want to unless their pursuits promise a better career. Readers will be surprised to know that when I was a high school teacher in New Delhi (India) for three years (between 2003 and 2007) almost every boy in my class wanted to become an engineer and go to the United States to settle down. This cannot be due to intrinsic motivation! I saw a deep conflict within children to meet the expectations of their parents. Unfortunately, as children succeed academically, they stop paying attention to their inner voice, and those who cannot meet the expectations of their parents consider themselves good for nothing. How ideals create conflict within children has already been discussed in this chapter.

When children are subject to deep conditioning, fragmentation occurs at various levels. As I noted above, conditioning influences come from various sources and often these sources are conflicting. Sexuality is part of biological conditioning, whereas religious teachings preach chastity. These contradictory positions bring about deep fragmentation of the psyche irrespective of the choice—suppression or indulgence—an individual makes. Besides, conditioning influences have played a major role in bringing about social fragmentation. Unquestionably, religious, nationalistic, racial, and ideological conflicts, to a large degree, can be attributed to conditioning influences that are also supported and executed by educational institutions.

Evidently, education becomes responsible for bringing about deep psychological fragmentation when it is primarily centered on the "training of mind" to cultivate "efficiency" with no attention to the bodily, emotional, aesthetic, and spiritual dimensions of children. Modern education explicitly overemphasizes the cognitive or the intellectual dimension and is potentially responsible for bringing about skewed development of children where intellect overrides every other dimension. Interestingly, overemphasis on intellect may not result in highly developed intellectuals either. On the contrary, imposition of a one-dimensional education on everybody is more likely to be accountable for breeding widespread mediocrity.

Moreover, contemporary educational institutions primarily focus almost entirely upon formal structures of communication (primarily language) in spite of the fact that in everyday life "communication...is a complete organismic response involving facial gestures, bodily postures, emotional mood, tacit understanding, and personal organic needs.... Thus, the curriculum goals are essentially divorced from the concrete biology of students" (Macdonald [1975c] 1995, 124). Since school and its activities are primarily centered upon developing "socially useful" human capacities, students as organisms are "disembodied" by means of subordinating bodily functions—erotic pleasure, elimination, and digestion—to "verbal learning goals" (124). Even when the body is recognized, it is primarily in the context of physical education, games, and skills. In Macdonald's ([1975c] 1995, 124) view,

> This divorcement of the verbal from the affect and psychomotor activity provides a highly useful control and sorting mechanisms for society, but in the process destroys the fabric of everyday living in the sense of full organismic participation in life. In the process it helps teach students to distrust their own values, emotions, and bodies as basic aspects of life and to this extent diminishes the full meaning of being alive.

The overemphasis on verbalism in most schools is also problematic because it is primarily concerned with "manipulating words whose referent is other words" instead of "connecting language activity to concrete experience, to self-expression in the act of full participation in [learning and] living." While there is no criticism of "the need of words about words" in schooling, the issue becomes significant because verbalism is "fundamental and pervasive throughout schooling." Verbalism, as it is operational now, is "essentially self-defeating since it rejects the building of language in concrete reality and divorces meaning structures from active potentials of human beings" (Macdonald [1975c] 1995, 124–125).

Neurologically, overemphasis on cognition results in more development of the left brain (intellectual), thereby leaving the right brain (creative) underdeveloped. Ken Robinson's (2001, 2009) assertion that schools kill creativity is a strong and valid allegation on the fragmentary approach of modern educational institutions. Overemphasis on "hard knowledge" (math and science) at the expense of the arts and humanities in contemporary schools is aptly described by Macdonald ([1971a] 1995, 40) as the "tyranny of knowledge."[6] The school curriculum in itself represents a fragmentary approach:

> The school curriculum over the years looks like a series of separately strung beads with no attempt to relate them to each other, and the consequent experience of students is of several varied and disconnected experiences which are often forgotten shortly after they are encountered. (Macdonald([1971a] 1995, 41)

Such a fragmented curricular orientation requires of teachers that they view their work in compartments. Guided by this scheme, each school discipline becomes an isolated entity in itself, which can further be broken down into a manageable units and sequence. Teachers are "competent," "accountable," and "interchangeable"; teaching is "measurable" and "reproducible"; and learning is according to a strict plan, mechanical, and quantifiable (Macdonald [1975c] 1995, 112). Macdonald explains further:

> This in effect detaches the work of students in school from their own sense of wholeness and experiential continuity. The quality of their engagement and the sense of control over their experience are submerged in the imposition and compartmental manipulations of their work experience.
>
> Inherent in this procedure is the technically rational planning and organization of work tasks and pupil activity which, in the interest of others, destroy spontaneity, creativity, playfulness, and essential risk-taking potentials of everyday living experiences. ([1975c] 1995, 122)

Governed by technological rationality, work for teachers and students is seen as divorced from their subjective lives, which brings about "dual identity," and in turn requires "internal psychological or emotional management" and strict outer disciplinary procedures (Macdonald [1975c] 1995, 113). Thus, "the activity of the schools," Macdonald explains, "represses the uniqueness of our own [subjective] meaning structures" (119).

It is the hierarchy of power and bureaucratic authority, use of reward and punishment, and the judgmental ethos of school processes that subjective expression and relationships are undermined. In such a controlled environment, it becomes risky for students and their teachers to express their personal meanings. Their only task is to carry out the goals set out by the administrators, politicians, and industrialists. In circumstances where individuals challenge the existing policies, school authorities use subtle and explicit repressive regulations. In most cases, children engage themselves in what Macdonald calls the "'forgetfulness' concerning their own meanings... they repress or submerge the unique meaning structure growing out of their own activity and take on the attitude and posture of the control agent" (119). Repressive forgetfulness, thus, leads to alienation—personal and social—that in turn leads to "withdrawal and passivity," "lack of initiative," and "anger and aggression" in the short term and "neurosis, psychosis, fanciful romantic nonsense, drug experience, and social violence" in the long term (119). Certainly, the cultivation of dual identity and effacing of subjectivity in educational experience is responsible for inward and outward fragmentation. *A fragmented education where some aspects are overstressed while others are left underdeveloped becomes responsible for the lopsided growth of children and the lack of capacity to deeply understand and resolve their psychological and relational conflicts.*

Certainly, when the primary focus of our educational institutions is the intellectual dimension, they are bound to serve the need of the industry without much concern for the inner beings of the individuals. There are, Krishnamurti (1982 in Thapan [1991] 2006, 17–18) points out, "two vital movements" in our lives:

> One stream is that of the technological world, the world of computers, of knowledge, the physical world with all its complications. The other stream is the psychological world with its conflicts, miseries, confusion, opinions, beliefs, dogmas, religious divisions, sorrows, pains, fears, a lack of integrity and so on. These two rivers are...life.

Our educational institutions, in most cases, have certainly overstressed the "technological or knowledge stream" at the expense of the "psychological stream." In the modern world where the emphasis on technical efficiency and professional expertise is almost fanatic, Krishnamurti (1953, 18) raises a tremendous question: "Will technique give us the capacity to understand life...The exclusive cultivation of technique has produced scientists, mathematicians, bridge builders, space conquerors; but do they understand the total process of life?" Moreover, will not emphasis on just one aspect, for example, professional training, lead to the development of lopsided personalities instead of integrated individualities? The case of a scientist can be a suitable example here. The training and ability to break an atom and to release atomic energy does not ensure the care of its appropriate use. "The man who knows how to split the atom," Krishnamurti (1953, 19) feels, "but has no love in his heart becomes a monster." If the society creates scientists whose thoughts and actions are not deeply integrated, scientific and professional training may be extraordinarily hazardous, as we have experienced over the centuries. *If education is merely concerned with training children to feed into systems of society, there could be little possibility for creative growth and integration among them and those who teach them.*

Undoubtedly, professional training is very important for the survival of society and for creative growth of individuals. However, professional training and achievements without self-understanding do not appear to be of great worth. "Surely," Krishnamurti (1964, 9) professes, "life is not merely a job, an occupation; life is something extraordinarily wide and profound, it is a great mystery, a vast realm in which we function as human beings." And the way to this mystery lies in never to "die inwardly." Krishnamurti (1999b, 26–27) argues,

> I think the function of right education is not only to help us to work hard—competently and efficiently—outwardly, but also to help us to never die inwardly. It is to help us have that extraordinary inward dynamo, that inward sense of tremendous activity that does not seek a result. Right education is the integration of activity—the inner and the outer."

Inner activity is a persistent inquiry into one's conditionings, ambitions, and desires and the ways in which the latter influence one's perceptions and actions. Certainly, the outer activity is very important, "but it is the inner activity," Krishnamurti (1999b, 27) points out, "which has much more significance, because it controls the outer. So education, it seems to me is to help us to not die inwardly."

Undoubtedly, given the state of the psychological and social fragmentation, one of the prime functions of education should be to cultivate a sense of deep integration within children, which is necessary for the awakening of intelligence and, which in turn, is essential for them to understand and transform themselves and their relationships.

CONCLUSION

The domain of education is deeply affected by and in turn affects the larger human consciousness. It is not hard to see how the characteristic features of human consciousness—fear, conditioning, becoming, and fragmentation—are reflected in and perpetuated through most contemporary educational institutions. More often than not, educational institutions cultivate fear through the imposition of discipline and authority; condition delicate minds by means of ideological, religious, and market propaganda; instill ambition and competitiveness; and fragment a child's being by overemphasizing on the cognitive aspect at the expense of emotional, bodily, creative, and spiritual dimensions. In short, contemporary educational institutions, in most cases, are responsible for negatively affecting the development of creativity, intelligence, and understanding among children, and do not provide ground for self-transformative teaching and learning.

By means of the previous two chapters I discussed two aspects of curriculum as meditative inquiry: first, human consciousness is in conflict; and second, educational institutions reflect and perpetuate conflicted nature of human consciousness. In the next chapter I discuss in detail the meaning and significance of meditative inquiry in the process of understanding and transforming human consciousness. In chapter 5, I will propose reimagining curriculum as a space for meditative inquiry that has the potential to help children and their teachers to engage in those educational experiences that support deeper self-understanding, creative expression, and transformation.

CHAPTER 4

ON THE NATURE OF MEDITATIVE INQUIRY

INTRODUCTION

In the previous two chapters I discussed two principles of curriculum as meditative inquiry: first, I argued that human conflicts—individual and social—are deeply connected to the nature of human consciousness characterized by fear and insecurity, conditioning and image-making, becoming and psychological time, and fragmentation and conflict; and second, I discussed how contemporary educational institutions, being part and parcel of human consciousness, reflect and perpetuate the latter's characteristic features. In this chapter I discuss the third principle: meditative inquiry. First, I analyze the limitations of thinking, analysis, systems, and authority in understanding and changing human consciousness. Then, I explain the meaning of meditative inquiry and its significance for psychological and social transformation.

LIMITATIONS OF THINKING AND ANALYSIS

Analysis and thinking—central features of intellectual pursuits—alone cannot solve human problems (Krishnamurti 1954). Why not? If you may recall the discussion about the process of "becoming" and "the observer and the observed," it would be easy to understand the limitations of thinking and analysis. Based on that discussion, *is not "the analyzer/observer/thinker/controller" also "the analyzed/observed/thought/controlled"*? If the very structure of thought is deeply conditioned, fragmented, and ridden with fear how can it understand and transform itself? Whatever understanding the thought or "I" will have through thinking and analysis will be beset with fear, fragmentation, and conditioning because thinking and analysis are not different from "thought" and "analyzed"; they are part of the same movement. Moreover, analysis is a never-ending process. If one tries to understand one's fear through analysis one will never be able to finish the process as there are so many kinds of fear.[1] "Is it possible," Krishnamurti asks, "to be aware...without analysis" (Krishnamurti and Smith 1996, 209)? Instead of analyzing one fear after another, it is important to observe fear as an existential phenomenon without naming it as "fear" or naming different kinds of fear.

Moreover, thought being the response of memory (which is based on the past, modifying itself into the present, and going into the future) can never directly meet any problem, which is always new, existentially speaking. In other words, since thought meets the challenge (present) with the memory (past), it is unable to have a direct and deeper perception into the problem. It translates the problem according to its conditioning and hence is unable to deal with it[2] (Krishnamurti 1983). It is not incidental that theories and philosophies and their proposals to solve human problems have become more important than the problems themselves. Thought has created all kinds of systems—religious, political, economic, educational, and technological—according to its conditioning to solve fundamental human problems. *But the nature of human psychological problems, which are also at the root of wider structural problems, is such that they cannot be solved from outside, at least to date they have not been.*[3]

Finally, thought reduces existential things into words through "verbalization" and "naming" and thus stops their comprehension (Krishnamurti 1954). For example, the comprehension of the feeling of anger or greed becomes extremely difficult if one translates these feelings into words. Language and words are necessary to communicate things to others, but within oneself the constant movement of thought functions as the constant verbalization of feelings, which is more of an escape than having a perception and understanding. Escape implies not coming into direct contact with the feelings. And when verbalization happens mechanically, it acts as a barrier between awareness and feelings. For example, when anger arises we may quickly translate the feeling of anger into the words—"I am angry"—and start fighting with it or getting along with it instead of being aware of it so that it may open itself up. Instead of verbalization, Krishnamurti suggests *self-awareness* or *pure observation* that involves neither translating the state of being into words nor judging it with predetermined ideals, but rather observing it with full attention.

A question that may arise in reader's mind is: Was Krishnamurti against thinking and analysis? Actually not. Consider Krishnamurti's responses to Chogyam Trungpa Rinpoche, renowned Buddhist teacher:

> *Krishnamurti(K)*: I inquire into disorder and I want to know why there is disorder, I do not want to find order, then I have all the gurus and all the gang coming in! I do not want order, I only want to find out why in one's life there is such chaos and disorder.
> *Chogyam Trungpa Rinpoche (CT)*: Well, you cannot find out intellectually.
> *K: Intellect is part of the whole structure, you cannot deny intellect.*
> *CT*: But you cannot use intellect to solve intellectual problems.
> *K*: No, you cannot solve these problems at any level except totally.
> (Krishnamurti and Rinpoche 1996, 238; emphasis added)

Krishnamurti was approached by highly educated people in the West as well as in the East.[4] Among his admirers were physicists, writers, Nobel laureates, scientists, psychiatrists, musicians, poets, artists, educators, and philosophers with whom Krishnamurti engaged throughout his life at the level of intellect—which, of course, was rooted in his deeper existential insights—to point out that although intellect and language are very important, there is a level of our existence, which can only be experienced and understood in the state of "pure observation." Consider Krishnamurti's words:

> There is another way [to self-inquiry] which is not the operation of the intellect. So far, this morning, [in these dialogues] we exercised our intellect, our thinking, and the very thinking pushed us step by step, deeper and wider; but it still was the movement of thought, the movement of time, of measure. The question [by the participant] is whether there is any inquiry which is not born out of remembrance and thought. I say there is... There is an action which is not the action of memory, of thought, of the intellect [and hence of knowledge], and that action is *pure observation*... You ask: what do you mean by "pure observation"?... *The description is not the described. The word is not the*

thing... Can we observe without the word? Can we observe our wives, our husbands, our daughters, or the tree, or the river, without the word?—for the word is not the thing. (1999b 147; emphasis added)

As I discussed previously, thinking, analysis, and division have their place in the dimension of material reality, but the problem starts when we extend the same processes to understand the nature of self or thought. Expressing it differently, *while intellectual understanding is very significant, extending it to the sphere of consciousness without realizing intellectual understanding's limitations is problematic.* For example, how will I understand my psychological states such as fear? Through somebody else's theories or my own ideas? I can begin there, but since fear is existential—not theoretical or intellectual—I will have to take an existential route; that existential route is meditation or pure observation, which is to look "at fear not as an abstraction, but actually at fear as it occurs" (Krishnamurti and Smith 1996, 206).

It may be a general concern among readers that in the situation where thought will be absent our life will be like death. That is not so. According to Krishnamurti, it is only with the cessation of the mechanical movement of thought—not the capacity of thinking, which Krishnamurti himself used throughout his life—that there is direct perception of reality, which brings about insight and intelligence (Krishnamurti and Bohm 1985, 1999; Bohm 1992).

SYSTEMS VIS-À-VIS CONSCIOUSNESS

If thinking and analysis cannot solve psychological problems, how can the various systems—religious, political, economic, educational, psychological, and social—that are based on thought? What is the problem with systems? Dependency on a system for any fundamental change inevitably involves hierarchy between the leader and the led, between those who know and have the power and those who do not know and are powerless. Moreover, change in the system merely represents a continuation of modified realities. Communism, for example, is nothing but modified capitalism with new hands that hold power and exploit.[5] Also, *change in a system is static; once it is carried out, for example, the formation of a law or a policy, it is not self-renewing or self-reflecting. On the contrary, the human psyche, which is the basis of all human actions and relationships, can constantly remain in change or transformation.* Thus, society in the latter sense would be a dynamic entity based on human relationships (rather than merely a set of structures), which would undergo constant transformation if people would be in transformation within themselves (Krishnamurti 1953; Krishnamurti and Anderson 2000). Krishnamurti (1953, 16) explains,

> Systems, whether educational or political, are not changed mysteriously; they are transformed when there is a fundamental change in ourselves. The individual is of first importance, not the system; and as long as the individual does not understand the total process of himself, no system, whether of the left or of the right, can bring order and peace to the world.

This stance is generally opposite to the existing conceptualizations regarding human conflicts and problems, especially the ones propounded by Marx and his adherents, as I also discussed previously. Marxist and neo-Marxist conceptualizations attribute human misery to capitalist system. While it is important to defy a capitalist system because it is based on exploitation, proposing communism as the alternative does not seem to be the best choice. Instead of being structure-oriented, what is far more significant is that each one of us goes to the very depths of our psychological reality—its contradictions, conflicts, and problems—to understand how we are part and parcel of this exploitative social reality, and how, knowingly or unknowingly, we are inheriting the existing system and contributing toward the increasing chaos.

It is important for each one of us to realize that no outside agency can bring about a total revolution of the psyche but the individual himself or herself, and unless there is a revolution in the psyche there can be no fundamental change in the society (Krishnamurti 1992; Krishnamurti and Anderson 2000). Here I am reminded of a question posed to me after my presentation (A. Kumar 2008a) by Steven Strauss, a neurologist by training and Marxist by ideology, at the Rouge Forum conference: How can critical self-awareness help us fight oppression? The crux of my response to his question was like this: *Perception is action; if you see the oppression and do not justify or escape you are bound to respond to the moment, not with a theory or ideology, but with the intelligence that comes with observing things as they are.*

Consider Krishnamurti's views regarding "seeing" and "action" when he explained the same issue to students and teachers of his school at Rajghat, India:

> To see everything as it is, is quite an art. It is as difficult to see things as they are as it is to learn mathematics, history, or geography. When you go out for a walk, you really do not see the squalor and misery of the poor, the filth on the road, and the diseased dog. If you begin to see all this, you would do something about it, and that is the beauty of seeing. *Seeing is action.* If you see, if you observe, if you listen, you cannot help but act. But most of us are blind and deaf, so we do not act. And when we do act, it is according to some idea and, therefore, there is conflict between the idea and the action. But if we began to see and listen, then out of that very seeing and listening there would be direct action. (1999b, 56–57; emphasis added)

I must clarify here that this understanding—perception is action—does not dispute the importance of structural changes. *Seeing is action* is not a support for anarchism. There is no denial to the view that systems, structures or laws could be of help. But the total reliance on systems for transformation indicates a lack of thoughtfulness and mutual understanding. The key issue that needs to be acknowledged is that change in the structures is not sufficient; we need to bring about change in the human psyche and thereby in the society it has created. *New structures are necessary but they should grow out of transforming consciousness, not fixed theories.*

Though anybody who believes in human subjectivity and agency will tend to agree that transformation of consciousness is important, some questions are still inevitable: What about the religious and political propaganda? What about hate speeches? What about thoughts and actions of insensitive people? What about technological and other changes? Does this idea of "psyche" over "system" mean that it doesn't matter much what "systems" people live in?

Certainly, there can be no denial to the extraordinary impacts systems have on the way people think, behave, and feel but it is important to question the idea that changing systems can bring about *radical change* in people's consciousness (Krishnamurti 1992). Systems actually are crystallized forms of our consciousness; the origin of our structures is rooted in our psychology.[6] The actuality is that there is consciousness as flux (the individual self) and as crystallized form with slow modifications (structures). *So any change in structures (crystallized consciousness), if it is to be substantial and profound, has to begin in the consciousness (self in flux) first.* If anybody thinks that changing the system can bring about a revolution of the human psyche, one is directly or indirectly accepting the notion that human beings need to be controlled from outside and that it is not human beings and their interactions that create systems but the other way round. Besides, the change that will occur in human psyche—say due to a change in a law against racism or casteism—may only superficially modify people's thinking about the problem of discrimination. The law or policy cannot make sure that people deeply realize the implications of hatred and discrimination. In fact, the very reason there are so many laws to avoid discord between individuals and groups clearly reveals to what extent we have depended on external forces to govern our beings from outside so that we may observe right behavior. And the saddest thing is that laws and rules are broken everywhere even by the people who very well know the implications of their actions.

Our systems—religious, political, economic, and educational—represent us. If our systems are oppressive and exploitative, they do not reveal so much about themselves as they do about us, who actually created them through our interactions. In a structural approach to change, human beings can be treated as machines to be organized and controlled by the outside authority. Surely, the latter scheme of thought contains in it totalitarian and fascist ways of approaching human problems. In my understanding we have created these systems, and now we are caught in our own creation. And not knowing what to do we have been focusing upon changing systems in spite of the fact that we have failed largely—politically, religiously, educationally, and economically. *Changing systems is essential for they are oppressive; but, is not merely changing the systems, without focusing on who brought them into existence in the first place, an exercise in self-deception?*

It is obvious to ask: Why does not Krishnamurti's own thought represent a system or theory? Krishnamurti never created a system of thought or proposed a theory. If one pays attention to what Krishnamurti says one will notice that he is not at all suggesting a system. On the contrary, he is urging us, if we like, to reconsider what we have created on the planet after thousands of years of evolution—biological, cultural, and scientific. The things that he is concerned with are self-understanding, intelligence, creative understanding of one's relationship to others, which are not based on a system, technique or formula. If someone asks me to summarize Krishnamurti's insights in a word, I would say: meditation or awareness. How could that form a system? At the level of language or semantics, awareness can be systematic for the sake of explanation, but in practice, existentially, it is inherently unsystematic (Pinar pers. comm.); "Truth," Krishnamurti (1929, para. 2) maintains, "is a pathless land." Krishnamurti wrote many books and talked to people all over the world to underscore the importance of self-awareness. Whatever there is in his books can be best described as the "negative approach," which is focused on understanding and negating what inhibits self-awareness.

THE PROBLEM OF AUTHORITY

Krishnamurti also rejects the idea of authority in bringing about psychological change. Perhaps Krishnamurti is the only person in the whole history of humankind who continuously talked of psychological transformation for about 60 years of his life but denied the role of authority in such a change including that of his own. Why? Because dependence on authority, whether of an outside agency or that of one's own self, cripples intelligence and creativity. What causes people to accept authority in the psychological sphere?

Since the self is in such flux and uncertainty, it seeks authority—either in religion, political ideology, a philosophical system or a psychological theory or in one's own idiosyncrasies—out of fear. People with authority, who claim that they "know," bring about exploitation of the common people by means of reward and punishment, control, suppression, and fear. The authority of one's own self is also problematic because the self that we have is conditioned and fragmented so it does not allow for a fresh perception in its own nature. *So methods and systems either imposed from outside or cultivated within cannot bring about the comprehension of the self* (Krishnamurti and Smith 1996). Notably, in this discussion on the problem of authority, there is absolutely no dispute regarding the importance of the authority of an expert in the technical fields, for example, language and music. The problem starts when we begin to depend on a figure of authority psychologically.

It is obvious to question: Why should not Krishnamurti be seen as the head of an authoritarian, hierarchical, and paternalistic system?

In most religious systems, there is clear a sense of authority. There is always a God, a savior, conceptions of hell and heaven, salvation, and all other sorts of things to demand its followers' faith. Krishnamurti was a radical teacher because of his emphasis on a complete break from the existing hierarchical and paternalistic religious orders. Organized religions and their political affiliations have always acted to make people lose their individuality and succumb to some higher authority.[7] Obviously, Krishnamurti too appears like others as he addressed huge masses of people and established foundations, schools, and study centers. He was trying to do the most difficult thing and must appear contradictory to those who have not tried to go deeper into his whole way of approaching human problems. He made "discoveries" into human beings' psychological sphere and tried his best to share them with as many people as he could (Bohm 1999, ix). Had what he been saying for almost 60 years of his life was clear to everybody, there would be no need for him to do what he did. His whole effort was to help us understand the crisis in our consciousness and be free of it to create a better world. He threw us on our own selves, and since he knew he was seen as a figure in authority he reminds us constantly in almost all of his talks that he should not be seen as an authority because *in the inner sphere and its transformation there can be no authority.* Consider Krishnamurti's stance regarding his authority:

> I do not demand your faith; I am not setting myself up as an authority. I have nothing to teach you—no new philosophy, no new system, no new path to reality; there is no path to reality any more than to truth. All authority of any kind, especially in the field of thought and understanding, is the most destructive, evil thing. Leaders destroy the followers and followers destroy the leaders. *You have to be your own teacher and your own disciple. You have to question everything that man has accepted as valuable, as necessary.* (1969, 21; emphasis added)

Krishnamurti (2005a, 126) explains further,

> There is no authority in these dialogues between us. The speaker has unfortunately to sit on a platform, but that does not give any authority. This is not a personality cult. And what he says is not something for you to think about and act on later. Here and now we are going together to explore and in so exploring act.

Krishnamurti discovered something invaluable in his own self, which he longed desperately to share with us. He never says accept his words; he only asks us to "consider together" and "test it out" if what he says has any truth (Krishnamurti [1979] 2005). If it has any then it is ours; for, *truth is not anybody's theory, which can be copyrighted. Truth belongs to the one who discovers it. And, fortunately we all can, at least, strive.*

Thought and analysis will not do nor will dependence on systems and authority. "What shall we do, then?" people would ask with bewilderment, for Krishnamurti takes away all their psychological crutches. In my view Krishnamurti's answer to the human problems constitute a single word that is tremendously meaningful and has infinite potential: *meditation.*

MEDITATIVE INQUIRY: THE KEY TO UNDERSTAND AND TRANSFORM HUMAN CONSCIOUSNESS

Human subjectivity, commonly understood to be constituted of memories, images, thoughts, emotions, and experiences, is much deeper. In fact, subjectivity-as-self or Ego, through its constant movement, does not allow for an inner experience of complete silence or freedom. This silence in which there is pure observation is not only necessary to have a profound understanding of one's own psychological movement but also that of one's relationship to people, property, and nature. *It is not "I," contrary to the common understanding, that allows for the experience of life; in actuality, "I," which is the abstracted entity from the constantly moving psychological images, obstructs the experience of reality: that which actually is.*

Undoubtedly, we need intellect, memory, feelings, and actions, for without them there will be no human existence. The real matter of concern is the abstracted entity "I" born of the thousands of fast moving images about itself and others, which, in actuality, brings about fragmentation within and forbids a deeper relationship with others. It is in order to have inward silence and profound outward communication and relationship that this constant movement of images, which is the basis of "I," must come to an end. What does it mean to end the "I" or the images? Does it mean that we should destroy our egos, as the religions have been teaching for thousands of years? Absolutely not. Krishnamurti meant something entirely different when he says "observe without observer or Ego." His main concern is that we meet life directly each moment rather than through the screen of our past experiences. If we look at life from the background of past experiences what we see is our own projection, which inhibits a clear perception of things as they are.

What is the method to meet life directly, inwardly as well as outwardly? Krishnamurti denied all methods and methodologies in the process of self-exploration, because they create a pattern that the mind then follows to achieve a desired result. Moreover, all systems and methods spring from and are influenced by thought, which is conditioned and fragmented. There are no steps, stages, or phases through which one can understand and end the movement of thought, for they are bound to be part of the thought itself. However, Krishnamurti did talk of inquiry—meditation—into the nature of thought, an inquiry that is not fixed and rigid but pliable and fluid. Consider this small excerpt of a dialogue between Krishnamurti and Houston Smith, professor of philosophy at the Massachusetts Institute of Technology:

> *Huston Smith (HS)*: [A]re you saying...that it is an inappropriate question to ask you how this lucidity [or the clarity of perception to live without conflict] is to be achieved?
>
> *Krishnamurti (K)*: No, not at all, sir. But the "how" implies...a method, a system. And the moment you have a system and a method you become mechanical, you just do what you are told. And that's not clarity. So to have clarity, the first essential thing is freedom from authority [of others, methods, and one's own conclusions].
>
> *HS*: And I feel in a kind of bind, because this freedom is attractive too and I want to go toward that, but I also want to pick your mind and ask you how to proceed? Am I moving away from my freedom if I ask you how to proceed?
>
> *K*: No, sir, but I am pointing out the difficulty...[T]he word "how" implies intrinsically a mind that says, please tell me what to do.
>
> *HS*: Yes. And I ask again, is that a mistaken question, is that a wrong question?
>
> *K*: I think that it is a wrong question...But rather if you say, what are the things, the obstructions that prevent clarity, then we can go into it. But if you say right from the beginning, what is the method— there have been a dozen methods and they have all failed, they have not produced clarity, or enlightenment, or a state of peace in man. On the contrary these methods have divided man; you have your method, and somebody else has his method, and these methods are everlastingly quarreling with each other.

HS: Are you saying that once you abstract certain principles and for-
mulate them into a method, this becomes too crude to meet the
intricacies?

K: That's right. The intricacies, the complexities and the living quality of clarity.

HS: Well, this is a hard teaching. It may be true and I am reaching
for it, and yet I don't know that it's possible—I don't feel that it's
possible completely to relinquish the question how and everything.

K: Sir, I think we shall be able to understand each other if we could
go a little slowly, not into the "how," but what are the things that
prevent clarity.

HS: All right, fine.

K: *Through negation... come to clarity, not through the positive method
of following a system.* (Krishnamurti and Smith 1996, 201–202;
emphasis added)

NEGATIVE APPROACH

The negative approach to understanding the nature of one's self is the
essence of meditative inquiry. To understand the significance of the
negative approach recall the previous discussion in the present chapter
where I pointed out the limitations of thinking, analysis, systems, and
authority—the central tenets of a positive approach. What is a positive approach?

> Being miserable, I want a way out; so I take a tranquilizer, or go to a
> guru, or to a church, or do some other foolish, ugly thing, and am satis-
> fied. That is the positive approach. It is the approach of a mind that is in
> conflict, that is in a state of sorrow, confusion, and that wants an answer,
> a way out—which it seeks through the practice of a method, a system, or
> through some other positive activity. (Krishnamurti 1991c, 292)

Essentially, a positive approach tries to comprehend a problem with
the help of a method, technique, or a system, which inevitably has to
be based on thought and memory. But the nature of existential problems—for example, fear—is such that they are always in the present;
and when they are approached with a method, which employs the past,
they are never comprehended in their totality. The only contribution
a method can make is to bring about "modification" in the existing
psychological state, which does not qualify as real change. Moreover,
a system always involves an authority that has invented it and knows

about it. While in the technical field, in the field of memory and intellect, it is undesirable to "reinvent the wheel," in the psychological sphere to depend on somebody or something is absolutely dangerous, for it cripples the creative intelligence that is required to understand the problem. *The beginning of creative intelligence lies in the negation of the positive—whatever has been invented and put together by thought—psychologically speaking.*[8] The mind that is interested in knowing itself fully never depends on what others have said or what one has thought about the self and its intricacies. Its only function is to understand that any positive action in the field of consciousness will bring about fragmentation, becoming, and conflict. "[I]t is only such a mind," Krishnamurti (1991c, 292) stresses, "which has torn everything apart [psychologically speaking], which is not seeking any form of satisfaction or gratification, which has no end in view" that can inquire into the depths of one's complexities.

Understanding this—that thought is fragmented, fearful, engrossed in becoming and conflict-ridden as well as having this perception that because of the preceding factors thinking, analysis, authority, and systems cannot bring about profound psychological transformation—is part of the negative approach. Negation helps remove the obstacles, which unburdens the mind, to observe the problem with full attention without any interference from thought. The positive—be it love or nonviolence—is not born through following ideals, which are opposite to the present state, but through thinking negatively and observing the present state of the mind. Consider Krishnamurti's ([1979] 2005, 171–172) statements:

> Is thought love? Does thought cultivate love? It is not pleasure, it is not desire, it is not remembrance, although they have their places. Then what is love? Is love jealousy? Is love a sense of possession, my wife, my husband, my girl—possession? Has love within it fear? It is none of these things, entirely wipe them all away, end them, putting them all in their right place—then love is.
>
> Through negation the positive is...But we, on the contrary, posit the positive and then get caught in the negative. One must begin with doubt—completely doubting—then you end up with certainty. But if you start with certainty, then you end up in uncertainty and chaos.

Significantly, the negative approach is not reactionary in nature. It is not a mere replacement of one approach for another. "If it [negative approach] is a reaction to the positive as communism is a reaction to capitalism," argues Krishnamurti, "then it is merely the same thing in a different form. *To change in the field of conditioning is not change at all*" (1991c, 292; emphasis added). He urges us to imagine ourselves to be in a desert alone. There is nobody, no theory, and no system. How will we understand our psychological nature? Obviously, self-awareness or self-observation is the only way left. In my understanding, the essence of the negative approach to self-knowledge is "meditation," "total attention," "pure observation," "self-awareness," or "understanding," which is key to comprehending and transforming one's consciousness.

WHAT IS MEDITATION?

Krishnamurti employs the word meditation in a completely different sense than its usual connotations. Usually, meditation implies an effort, a practice, and repetition of certain mantras or systems to deliberately calm the mind. In Krishnamurti's (1991b) view meditation is an effortless or *choiceless awareness* of one's self in relationship to ideas, people, and nature from moment to moment. In this awareness, which is passive in nature and where thought is not creating a division in itself, the problem reveals its true content and drops away on its own accord. This kind of awareness gives rise to an understanding or perception into the nature of things as they are without any distortion due to one's past experiences, memories, and images.

Such a perception or awareness requires careful listening and pure observation—the key elements of meditative inquiry. Meditative listening involves neither acceptance nor rejection but a "flowering"— letting the questions, ideas, and comments blossom and wither away. Listening is not only directed to the other participant/s but also to one's own self and to the surroundings. Thus, listening does not imply resistance and exclusion but a meditative awareness of the whole situation. It is important to clarify that listening is not against thinking, but it is critical for an intimate communication that listening should happen with a silent mind so that the listener does not project his own mind on what is being said (Krishnamurti 1991a; Krishnamurti and Anderson 2000). If the latter happens then one listens to one's own noise rather than to what is being said. Krishnamurti (1954, 10) explains,

There is an art of listening. To be able really to listen, one should abandon or put aside all prejudices, preformulations and daily activities. When you are in a receptive state of mind, things can be easily understood; you are listening when your real attention is given to something. But unfortunately most of us...are screened with prejudices, whether religious or spiritual, psychological or scientific; or with our daily worries, desires and fears. And with these for a screen, we listen. Therefore, we listen really to our own noise, to our own sound, not to what is being said.

The emphasis on listening might appear simplistic for everybody appreciates careful, active, and empathetic listening. But *listening is meditation*. I myself struggled to understand for quite a while as to why there is so much emphasis on listening for it is so obvious. The extraordinary importance of listening became clear to me while reading Krishnamurti's dialogues with David Bohm in *The Ending of Time* and with Allan Anderson in *A Wholly Different Way of Living* where Krishnamurti suggests that any act done with total attention, especially listening, ends the movement of thought! Besides, and here it gets even more profound, *when one listens to something or someone without the interference from the constant movement of thought the division between the listener and the speaker or the source of sound falls; they become part of the whole where two things—the origination of the sound and the act of listening—are happening simultaneously.* This is, of course, something for one to explore on one's own.

Before I discuss the meaning and significance of "pure observation," it is important that I clarify one possible conflation here regarding the term "observation." Krishnamurti uses the word "observation" in two different ways, which are rather opposite. In the first usage, Krishnamurti distinguishes between "the observer and the observed" to explain the problem of becoming and psychological time and the resultant conflict, as I discussed previously. In this kind of "observation" one part of "thought or Ego" ("observer") is separating itself from another part ("observed") leading to inward conflict and waste of energy. In the second usage, "observation" is equivalent to undirected or choiceless awareness or meditation. That is, to observe the movement of self without the interference of "I" or the movement of thought. In this observation there is no "I" or "observer" that is observing, but only pure observation. In other words, *observation in the latter sense implies to observe the outside objects and the way self operates without the observer, which means an observation where there is no ideal, comparison, judgment, control, or condemnation except for a choiceless awareness.* Krishnamurti explicates further:

> Have you ever experimented with looking at an objective thing like a tree [or the state of your mind] without any of the associations, any of the knowledge you have acquired about it, without any prejudice, any judgment, any words forming a screen between you and the tree [or your psychological state] and preventing you from seeing it as it actually is? Try it and see what actually takes place when you observe...with all your being, with the totality of your energy. In that intensity you will find that there is no observer at all; there is only attention. It is when there is inattention that there is the observer and the observed. *When you are looking at something with complete attention there is no space for a conception, a formula or a memory.* (1969, 90; emphasis added)

This observation without the observer allows a real perception of what is observed, outwardly and inwardly. Psychologically, such a pure observation also reveals the hidden layers of thought and facilitates understanding and insight into the nature of our psychological problems. Notably, such an understanding is not some final state to be achieved; it is an exploration into the "endless river" of one's consciousness. *It is this understanding of one's thought processes and one's relationship to people, ideas, and nature, rather than philosophies and theories, that has the potential to resolve individual psychological problems, which are also at the core of our collective problems.* What are the possible psychological and social implications of the disappearance of the division between "observer" and the "observed," inwardly as well as outwardly?

First, with the cessation of "the observer and the observed" contradiction one comes in direct contact with the psychological state, such as fear, without division between the "observer" and the "observed." Second, one experiences a real relationship with people, property, and nature based on direct contact with the object of attention instead of its images. Moreover, this real contact within and without dissolves the conflicts, which were in place due to images about oneself and another. For example, if a Pakistani can see an Indian and vice versa without the historical, cultural, and psychological divisions in place due to thick conditioning, the conflict can be eliminated for they both are part of the whole, existentially speaking. *The difference as division is a psychosocial construct.* Finally, the false division between human beings and the nature and universe falls and one becomes "holistic"— existentially, not theoretically—in the true sense of the word. In other words, by developing astute self-awareness one becomes capable of comprehending and ending psychological and social problems that are rooted in fear and insecurity, conditioning and image-making, becoming and psychological time, and fragmentation and conflict. It may be pointed out that Krishnamurti and Bohm (1986) also think that due to the cessation of conflict between the "observer" and the "observed" within one's self, the brain becomes silent and comes in contact with the Mind or the whole, which is the source of order, intelligence, love, and creativity that is free of the disorderly thought processes.

Two questions can be explored here. First: Do such experiences ever happen to anyone? Such a pure observation happens to each one of us when we face something unexpected such as a beautiful flower or a snow-clad mountain peak or are deeply interested in something such as a great musical piece or in situations when the self is completely absent in the action such as while dancing or playing music. Interestingly, Krishnamurti and Bohm (1986) and Bohm (1992) also think that what we call scientific insights also occur when the brain is in a rather silent and receptive state. "Eureka" is nothing but a form of insight. But such experiences or insights are usually momentary or like flashes, for as soon as thought recognizes them, which is past, insights become part of the general thought processes, which, then, instead of providing further insights becomes the barrier between the fact and the observation and thereby stops direct perception. So for a brain to live with insight rather than the mechanical thought, a meditative state is an important concern. *Subjectivity-as-self—bundle of memories, experiences, thoughts, and images about oneself, nature, and others—in this sense is a site of the conflict between the observer and the observed as well as a barrier between itself and whole or between the brain and the Mind.*

In their concern about the limitations of the particular or subjective, Krishnamurti and Bohm (1985) suggest that it is gravely important to move from the particular (subjective) to the general, psychologically speaking, (e.g., understanding that there may be so many fears in one's self due to various factors but the feeling of fear is the same. Moreover, fear is not only a particular thing within one's own self but is also a general feature of human consciousness) and from general to beyond. Krishnamurti explains to Bohm in *The Ending of Time*:

> From the particular, it is necessary to move to the general; from the general to move still deeper, and there perhaps is the purity of what is called compassion, love and intelligence. *But that means giving your mind, your heart, your whole being to this inquiry.* (Krishnamurti and Bohm 1985, 268; emphasis added)

This "beyond" is not far but in the very essence of "what is." *In this sense "worldliness" and "transcendent" are not opposite of each other; they are two aspects of the same reality, very much like matter and energy are.*

For 60 out of the 90 years of his life, Krishnamurti was constantly engaged with people, scholars, teachers, and students the world over to consider that unless "beyond" or "whole" operates through the narrow selves—fragmented, fearful, ambitious, competitive, conditioned—there can be no resolution to human psychological problems, which are also at the root of social, economic, and environmental problems. Nevertheless, one primarily functions through the brain so any idea about whole or Mind is still a projection of the brain. That is why Krishnamurti always emphasized an awareness of one's subjectivity rather than thinking about what is "beyond" or what happens when the brain comes in contact with the Mind. He leaves the latter for individual experimentation. The way to "beyond" lies not in thinking about beyond but "learning about oneself" (Krishnamurti and Bohm 1986, 87). *Thus self-knowledge—not only of the self we know but also of the self we do not know—is not optional but most essential.*

Second: Is it really possible to experience a radical change[9] in one's psychology and one's relationships with people and nature through cultivating self-awareness? In response to this question one must ask oneself: Am I really interested in understanding every bit of my being? Explicitly or implicitly, most of us are interested in self-fulfillment, ambitions, and at the same time we also try to cultivate the virtues of humility, nonviolence, and peace. All these do not qualify for self-transformation. *Self-transformation happens through self-awareness and self-understanding, which is to look within oneself to face as one is.* Most of us do not want to look within ourselves; if we *do* we want to adjust the conflicted thought processes into some workable self to carry on with our life of ambition and success. *Self-awareness has only one purpose, which is to live with such challenging questions as these: Is it possible to change our psychological nature radically? Can we listen and observe without interference from thought? Can the brain be completely silent? Can one be free of the conditioning, fear, fragmentation, and becoming?* These are not questions that need to be answered intellectually, for in answering we will either deny or assert. What is important is to live with these questions and see if these have any impact on the way we lead our lives.

CONCLUSION

By means of the present and the previous chapters I shared three principles of understanding curriculum as meditative inquiry: the nature of human consciousness, the problems of contemporary education, and the nature of meditative inquiry. As human beings we have myriad conflicts and problems at every level and sphere of our lives, which, knowingly or unknowingly, we have also extended to the entire planet. On the surface our problems may appear to have different reasons, but the majority of them are tied to the nature of our consciousness. Meditative inquiry is a possible way, especially when most of our methods to change humanity have largely failed, to investigate our consciousness to see if the fear, conditioning, becoming, and fragmentation can be dissolved to bring about a holistic and integrated human being. In the next chapter I propose—based on my study of the curriculum theory of Macdonald and educational insights of Krishnamurti—to reimagine curriculum as a space of meditative inquiry into one's own self and one's relationship to people, property, and nature that may provide self-transformative experiences to students and their teachers.

CHAPTER 5

ON THE NATURE
OF CURRICULUM AS
MEDITATIVE INQUIRY

INTRODUCTION

Contemporary educational institutions, which are beset with and perpetuate fear, becoming, conditioning, and fragmentation, are unquestionably dangerous for the creative growth and development of children. Recognizing the problematic nature of modern education, I want to propose reimagining curriculum as a space for meditative inquiry, which is primarily concerned with developing what Krishnamurti calls "awareness" and what Macdonald calls "centering" among children and teachers, so that they may understand and transform their psychological nature and thereby society. According to Krishnamurti (1953, 46), the right kind of education

> should help the student to recognize and break down in himself all social distinctions and prejudices, and discourage the acquisitive pursuit of power and domination. It should encourage the right kind of self-observation and the experiencing of life as a whole, which is not to give significance to the part, to the "me" and the "mine," but to help the mind to go above and beyond itself to discover the real.

Echoing Krishnamurti's concerns Macdonald ([1964] 1995, 17) writes,

> [M]an has a personal, self-actualizing and creative capability not limited solely by biology or conditioning; that personal response is the

avenue through which individuals stretch and reach their potentialities; and that a view of human development which wishes to focus upon human potentialities must centre upon the development aspect of personal responsiveness... [which, according to Gordon Allport (1955), constitutes]... "self-aware, self-critical and self-enhancing capacities."

In this chapter, drawing upon the educational insights of Macdonald and Krishnamurti, I conceptualize a vision of curriculum that aspires, on the one hand, to undermine factors of fear, becoming, conditioning, and fragmentation and, on the other hand, to cultivate the development of personal responsiveness, openness, creativity, awareness, transcendence, and centering.

PERSONAL RESPONSIVENESS, OPENNESS, AND THE REALITY-CENTERED SCHOOL

Krishnamurti (1953, 1964) and Macdonald ([1964] 1995) think that society, through its incessant conditioning mechanisms, greatly undermines the quality of creative and critical response among children to respond to the inner (biological and psychological) and the outer challenges. In Macdonald's ([1964] 1995) view the fulfillment of the minimal conditions (i.e., physical growth and learning of social signs and symbols) is necessary but not sufficient for the development of "personal responsiveness." Social conditions, according to Macdonald ([1964] 1995), are "essentially *closed*" (19) in nature. "No matter what the structure of a specific culture may be," Macdonald explains, "the individual is closed in its symbolic universe and world view, its customs and mores, its functions and objects" (19). Therefore, while biological maturation and socialization are important, the development of personal responsiveness requires what Macdonald calls "openness to life." *Openness* to life is the "maximal condition for developing human potential" (20). It implies to be "open in thought" (fluent, flexible, and original), "open in affect" (experiencing the potential feelings in an activity), and "open in perception" (meeting the potential stimuli in the world). Significantly, this "openness"—a tremendous contribution from Macdonald's vision to the discipline of education—is not merely cognitive; it also encompasses the affective and perceptual dimensions. Do our contemporary schools facilitate the development of openness and personal responsiveness?

Based on the discussion on the nature of education previously, it seems reasonable to argue that the common philosophy of most contemporary schools is to encourage fear, becoming, conditioning, and fragmentation and, thereby, inhibit openness and personal responsiveness. Resonating Krishnamurti's view, Macdonald ([1964] 1995, 26) thinks that schools, via an "imposition of authority," establish absolute standards of "good" and "bad," "right" and "wrong" instead of relatively open concepts like "appropriate" and "inappropriate." The imposition of absolute standards of "good" and "bad" instead of a relative understanding of "appropriateness" or "inappropriateness" closes "alternatives in the development process" and stultifies "individual judgment." Since most of our schools are basically grounded on a "reward and punishment system" (Krishnamurti 1953), children generally tend to move along the predetermined standards and are thus embedded (Macdonald [1964] 1995).[1] "Learning," therefore, "becomes an affect-embedded necessity to maintain balance by escaping [punishment,] shame, guilt, anxiety, and seeking socially approved satisfaction and gratification" (28). *Naturally, imposition of authority and cultivation of fear undermines qualities of openness and personal responsiveness.*[2] Krishnamurti could not agree more with Macdonald, as is clear from my discussion on fear previously.

Instead of giving a "prescription" (Freire 1973, 47) of what is "right" or "wrong," Macdonald appeals to teachers to engage their students in a *value clarification process*—"a questioning behavior which is essentially non-judgmental and which does not reject pupils' answers." The main goal of this pedagogic approach is to help students be self-reflective of their thinking, assumptions, and values (Macdonald [1964] 1995, 29). Such a dialogical pedagogy requires teachers who demonstrate active, nonjudgmental and engaged listening, congruence in behavior (that implies a teacher is without any false pretense and meets his or her students person to person, not status to person), empathy (the ability to understand and feel students' meanings rather than making evaluative judgments), and positive regard toward thoughts and feelings of students. Macdonald's concern for this humanistic pedagogy, which he drew upon the work of Carl Rogers (1961, 1962) is, indeed, consistent with Krishnamurti's approach to education that is based on love, care, and understanding.

The school that gives space to openness, dialogue, responsiveness, and humanistic relations between teacher and learner[3] "is not child-centered or society-centered, or subject-matter centered. It is *reality-centered*" (Macdonald [1964] 1995, 32; emphasis in original):

> [S]chool does not exist primarily to inculcate our cultural heritage, not principally to develop role players for society, nor primarily to meet the needs and interests of learners. The school exists to bring learners in contact with reality, of which our society, ourselves, and our cultural heritage are parts.

The basic goal of a reality-centered school and its curriculum is founded upon the principle that children are self-actualizing. It sets learners free to explore, seek, search, discover, invent, and experiment. The teacher's role in a reality-centered school is to guide, clarify, help, and support the children. The reality-centered school is an "open" school[4] where children are seen as self-actualizers and creators, and the goal of learning is primarily to develop their capacities of "openness" and "responsiveness." "Reality-centered school," Macdonald maintains, "recognizes that *living is learning and the quality of living is the quality of learning*" ([1964] 1995, 33; emphasis in original). That is, "living" and "learning" are not mutually exclusive domains. In fact, it is the perceptive understanding of how one lives—thinks, feels, and acts—that constitutes learning rather than mere passive information absorption. The more deeply one understands one's living, the more perceptively and insightfully one learns.

FREEDOM, AESTHETICS, AND LOVE

Underscoring the significance of "personal responsiveness," "openness," and the "reality-centered school" is recognizing the tremendous importance of subjectivity in the educational process. Contemporary educational institutions however, because of primarily being based on technical rationality (the core of positivistic-behaviouristic-administraive-institutional-managerial-technocratic-standardized-scientific thinking), have overemphasized production of scientists and technologists and their supportive personnel who are organized into complex bureaucratic structures and thereby have greatly undermined the importance of individuality and "creative humanness." Thus, the majority of our schools have become an integral cog in our technocratic system as exemplified by the prevalence of alienation, boredom,

law and order, regimentation, and depersonalization in their overall
working (Macdonald [1971b] 1995, 50). The basic contradiction with
which our society and schools are beset, Macdonald argues,

> resides in the paradox of the immense promise for individual happi-
> ness and well-being inherent in technological society which is being
> paid for by the dehumanization of the individual for whom the prom-
> ise exists. Thus, we speak the rhetoric of progress at the sacrifice of
> humanity. (50)

In what ways, specifically, are individuals dehumanized in schools?
The dehumanization is primarily carried out by means of organizing educational experience around the "accumulative consumption
ideology of schools" (Macdonald [1975c] 1995, 122) or "ideology of
achievement"—"becoming" or "ambition" in Krishnamurti's terms,
as I discussed previously—that justifies grouping practices, testing
programs, grading, reporting, scheduling, and most of the current
school practices (Macdonald [1971b] 1995, 51).

The ideology of achievement, naturally, is based on the principles of
behaviorism, scientism, and psychologism where students are "learners" who have to be "motivated" and "measured," and who possess
certain "traits," "capacities," and "needs," which educators "diagnose"
(Macdonald [1971b] 1995, 52). Tests (standardized and otherwise)
in schools represent the grossest manifestations of the ideology of
achievement. Tests are justified all over the world because they "facilitate learning" through feedback and reinforcement. However, few
teachers and administrators seem to bother about the question: What
is the intrinsic value of conducting tests in terms of the growth and
development of children? According to Macdonald ([1971a] 1995),

> [S]tudents are taught their abilities by continuous evaluation and
> allotted social slots on the basis of their cumulative performance. This
> provides a useful way for society to deal with young as they emerge
> into the work force, for we can be assured that their predictive success
> (in terms of tests) has been set (psychologically and socially) as early as
> fourth or fifth grade. (42)

Guided by the "ideology of achievement," the "best" curriculum is
thought to be the one that is devoted to the realization of the collective
goals and the content of which is measurable, specific in detail, and

emphasizes the academic knowledge and skills necessary for collective needs—primarily reading, mathematics, and science (Macdonald [1971b] 1995, 54). In essence, technological rationality—"irrational rationality" (Macdonald [1981a] 1995)—predominates in schools and is "characterized by a complete commitment to an instrumental thinking which separates means from ends,...emphasizes the efficiency and effectiveness of measurable achievement and divorces human activity from the source of valued meanings or qualities" (162).

Even teachers who work under the influence of the ideology of achievement "teach from textbooks, manuals, and, if possible, from commercial plans. Teachers teach [homogenous] groups of children because it is easier to do so " (Macdonald [1971a] 1995, 44). Teachers even experience their own growth and development in terms of quantity of courses and credentials instead of qualitative changes in their personal and professional dimensions.

Certainly, such a behavioral and technological rhetoric has the effect of lifting the burden of our moral responsibility to children and freeing them for self-responsible and self-directed fulfillment of their own emerging potential (Macdonald [1971b] 1995, 52). Undoubtedly, as educators, it is our fundamental and moral responsibility not to succumb to the "ideology of achievement" and work as an "accountable technician" for the collective. On the contrary, we should help children in developing their full individual potential.

How can we make sure that individuals remain at the core of the educational process? First of all, we need to draw students' and teachers' attention toward the dominant "cultural mind-set" of the ideology of achievement. Macdonald ([1981a] 1995, 162) considers it necessary that

> [students and teachers]...see where it [technological rationality or ideology of achievement] enters...[their] lives through such practices as behavioral objectives, behavioral modification, and management by objectives, systems analysis, teacher competency approaches, and accountability movements. They must be constantly encouraged to shift from the "How?" to the "What?" and the "Why?"

Second, we must realize that "freedom" is a fundamental requirement in children's self-actualization. It is the presence of freedom and individuality that gives rise to "purposefulness"[5] in life (Macdonald [1964] 1995, 18). Thus, children need to be given the space to make efforts on their own and have experiences so that they can choose and be free of the constraints of the environment and their own internal structures (Macdonald [1971b] 1995, 53).[6]

In other words, education should help children to question and go beyond conditioning influences in and about them. In the absence of freedom, children will only conform to the conditions set by the society and breed mediocrity (Krishnamurti 1953). If we could emphasize creative self-understanding, instead of forcing the conditioning and the ideology of achievement, the former will naturally allow for the growth and development of one's personal interests and unique approaches to pursue and nurture those interests that may ultimately flower into one's vocation or profession. The development of self-understanding has the potential to question and resist the conditioning influences and the ideology of achievement, which inhibit creativity and intelligence.

Finally, we must bring back the aesthetic dimensions of education—humanities, the arts, literature, philosophy, and other aspects of social studies—that are slowly being pushed out of the school curriculum to the desert of irrelevancy because they cannot easily be included in the rhetoric of the ideology of achievement (Macdonald [1971b] 1995, 54–55). It is the aesthetic dimension that can act as a "counter culture" (Roszak 1970) and become a vehicle for providing a broadened freedom for the development of individual potentiality and of aesthetic relations to the world. Why aesthetics? In Macdonald's ([1971b] 1995, 57) view,

> The humanities [arts, literature, and philosophy] as a counter culture in the schools are focused squarely upon development of individual persons as human beings, upon welding of feeling and thought with action, and upon the awareness, experiencing, and analysis of cultural forms as expressive symbols. The validation of the truth of the humanities lies within the process of creating personal meaning in experiences, not in experimental abstractions and manipulations.

Aesthetics broadens the meaning and implications of rationality; it brings in emotions and creativity with intellectual activity. Endorsing John MacMurray's (1958, 47) assertion that "unless the emotions and intellect are in harmony, rational action will be paralyzed," Macdonald ([1971b] 1995, 56) defines rationality as "an integrated activity" that encompasses actions, thoughts, feelings, values, commitments, and involvement. Macdonald's concerns unquestionably resemble Krishnamurti's emphasis on holistic education.

Viewed from the perspective of aesthetics, curriculum, and pedagogy, thus, should be seen as creative expressions of human potential. In Macdonald's ([1971b] 1995) understanding, no specific theory, ideology, or research result can provide an absolute structure that is best for making a curriculum. These processes are the ways of science and technological rationality and are not amenable to the phenomena of curriculum—"a creative characteristic form involving selection and organization of symbols from many diverse areas... [where] all data that are relevant to concrete phenomena are welcomed... [and] are essentially assessed by aesthetic criteria" (58). This aesthetic approach to curriculum is "curriculum imagination" (60) where every aspect of school is engaged imaginatively. Macdonald elaborates further:

> There is no master plan; no secret of structuring subject matter; no secret formula for relating to others; no special methods of teaching the sciences or the humanities that are not inherent in the activity and substance themselves... Each situation is entered anew with the serious attitude of freedom and choice, with the goal of providing maximum opportunity for all to engage freely in meaningful doing through self-expressive activity in each new context. (60–61)

Mirroring Macdonald's concerns, Krishnamurti also thinks that there is no teaching or testing method by which to educate a child to be integrated and free. In fact, methods, which classify children according to temperament and aptitude, merely emphasize their differences, breed antagonism, encourage divisions among children as well as in society and do not contribute to developing integrated human beings. Dependence on a particular method of teaching or testing, rather than learning from present situations, indicates sluggishness on the part of the educator. "As long as education is based on cut-and-dried principles," Krishnamurti (1953, 23–24) claims, "it can turn out men and women who are efficient, but it cannot produce creative human beings."

Significantly, educators who are interested in awakening children's creative intelligence will lay far more emphasis on deeply understanding themselves and their pupils rather than depending on a new method of education. "When one follows a method," Krishnamurti (1953, 26) contends, "even if it has been worked out by a thoughtful and intelligent person, the method becomes very important, and the children are important only as they fit into it. One measures and classifies the child, and then proceeds to educate him [her] according to some chart." Obviously, method-centric education works well for the nation-states, the market, and management for its purpose is to produce, distribute, and sell educational commodities at the expense of spontaneous, creative, and rich experiences whereby the educator and the educated may grow into integrated beings.

No master plans, no methods, no specific theory, ideology or research! What is it that we teach children with, then? "Only love," Krishnamurti (1953, 24) suggests, "can bring about the understanding of another. Where there is love there is instantaneous communion with the other, on the same level and at the same time." Surely, it is in the absence of love, care, and respect for each other that we resort to an outside agency—government, system, philosophy, and ideology—to decide what and how we should teach. No government, market, organized religion, and even family is interested in children *as they are*; everybody's main concern is to seek control over education to meet their respective agenda. Krishnamurti (1953, 25) argues, "To study a child one has to be alert, watchful, self-aware, and this demands far greater intelligence and affection than to encourage him [her] to follow an ideal [or method]." In Krishnamurti's understanding, self-aware and integrated educators will come to the context-relevant technique or method "through experiencing, for the *creative impulse makes its own technique—and that is the greatest art*" (1953, 47; emphasis added).

TRANSCENDENCE, CENTERING, AND AWARENESS

While freedom, aesthetics, and love are very important as far as creative teaching, learning, and self-expression are concerned, a deeper understanding of self requires a profound search: a search for the "transcendental" (Macdonald [1974] 1995) and "beyond" (Krishnamurti and Bohm 1985) through "centering" (Macdonald [1974] 1995) and "meditation" (Krishnamurti 1954). In other words, *educational experience must incorporate a search for the spiritual dimensions of human beings so that students and their teachers not only have knowledge of the outer but also of the inner.* Why is knowledge of the inner—self-knowledge—so important?

Knowledge is not simply things and relationships that are real in the outer world and waiting to be discovered, but it is also a process of "personalizing" the outer world through the inner potential of human beings as that potential interacts with outer reality (Macdonald [1974] 1995, 83).[7] According to Macdonald (1966a, 4),

> Personal knowledge brings depth to meaning and reflects unique-ness of our own experience. The connotation we bring to words, the commitment we give to certain ideas, or the perceptual selections we make from among relevant alternatives are all predicated upon and integrated through the unique being of each individual.

The concept of "tacit dimension of knowledge" and its derivative "that we can know more than we can tell" (Polanyi 1967 quoted in Macdonald [1974] 1995, 84) explains this point further. Any "explicit knowing" (whether in practical and formal knowledge structures or in aesthetic and scientific realms) is grounded in a tacit dimen-sion of knowing (or understanding)—what Polanyi (1967) calls "indwelling"—that makes sense of explicit statements. Thus, "an epis-temology that does not recognize tacit knowledge components...is simply weighted down with the baggage of philosophical and materi-alistic biases" (Macdonald [1974] 1995, 86). It is the recognition of a tacit dimension—or what I call subjectivity-as-awareness—that forms the basis of transcendental, and in turn, meditative education.[8] From a transcendental perspective, what is most significant as an educational experience is the understanding of one's own inner being or what Macdonald, borrowing from Mary Caroline Richards (1962), calls "centering." What is centering as the goal of a meditative education?

Centering is a human experience facilitated in many ways by what Carl Jung calls "religious attitude"—not necessarily related to any recognizable creed—that encompasses the search to find our inner being or to complete one's awareness of wholeness and meaning as a person.[9] The process of centering draws its power and energy from the sources that are not completely explicable or what Krishnamurti calls "unknown" or "beyond." Centering is not in contradiction with the accumulated knowledge of a culture; it however places knowledge at the base or ground from which it grows. Thus centering is the funda-mental process of human beings that makes sense out of our percep-tions and cognitions of reality. In conclusion, the process of centering aims for the completion of the person or the creation of meaning that utilizes all the potential given to each person (Macdonald [1974] 1995, 86–88). Macdonald articulates the following questions as the core of an educational process that aims at centering:

> What kinds of activities are encouraged that provide for opening up perceptual experiences? What kinds of activity facilitate the process of sensitizing people to others, to inner vibrations? What kinds of activity provide experiences for developing close-knit community relationships? What kinds of activity encourage and facilitate religious experiences? What kinds of activity facilitate the development of patterned meaning structures? What ways can we organize knowledge to enlarge human potential through meaning? How can we facilitate the development of inner strength and power in human beings? (88)

In a nutshell, what should be the curricular and pedagogical considerations of a meditative education aimed at centering? Macdonald has given many brilliant suggestions to facilitate the process of centering in a thoughtful, engaging, and interesting manner that include: playfulness, meditative thinking, imagining, the aesthetic principle, the body and the biology, understanding of ecology, and education for perception.

Playfulness is the essence of an education that aims at centering. However, *work* is too often considered separate from *play* in the serious business of schools. The serious business of schools is conducted in linear, prescriptive, and restrictive *time* and *space*. *Materials* (school infrastructure, resources for teaching and learning etc.) are also strictly work-specific and are used in administratively prescribed ways. *Interactions and associations*—the approved process of communication and grouping practices—are also work-specific, prescribed, and "facilitative" of the learning. While *sexuality* is carefully repressed, it is utilized in its "bisexual implications" (Macdonald's term) for many managerial-disciplinary tasks such as the lining up of boys and girls for different activities. *Learning* in schools, thus, happens by working (not playing) in pre-decided interactions and associations, with predetermined materials in specific spaces under carefully controlled time sequences[10] (Macdonald [1977a] 1995, 131–132). The idea of *playfulness* is often seen as diametrically opposite to *seriousness* in most of our schools. Emphasis on playfulness implies that students are given freedom to play with ideas, things, and other people in a manner that does not make learning a burden. The reason for emphasizing playfulness is to provide freedom to children and their teachers so that they may learn creatively without any behaviorist and totalitarian disciplinary structure. *Playfulness is not against order; it is against a regimented structure that kills freedom, intelligence, and creativity.*

Meditative thinking[11] has the potential to make playful learning intelligent and sensitive. Instead of thinking in a functional, utilitarian, and a problem-solving manner, we should encourage what Heidegger (1966) called a "releasement toward things" and an "openness" to mystery. Emphasis on meditative thinking—rather than "calculative thinking"—encourages students not to accept things on their face value. It is our responsibility as educators that by means of meditative thinking we "encourage the young to say both yes and no to culture [or what Krishnamurti calls 'conditioning influences'] and probe the ground from which our culture arises " (Macdonald [1974] 1995, 92).

Evidently, meditative thinking and what Krishnamurti (1953) calls the "flame of discontent" in children is suppressed through giving them ambitions and ideals, conditioning them with political and religious dogmas, and cultivating in them fear of authority, discipline, failure, and rejection. If we, educators, are really interested in the development of "critical alertness and keen insight" among children then we must encourage them "to question the book, whatever it be, to inquire into the validity of the existing social values, traditions, forms of government, religious beliefs and so on" (41–42).

Most of us are afraid of meditative thinking or deep discontent, for it has the capacity to disturb false values, securities and comforts, and certainty in relationships and possessions. Instead of being afraid of discontent and canalizing it into a certain direction to avoid it, Krishnamurti (1964, 39) suggests to students that they "give it [discontent] nourishment until the spark becomes a flame and you are everlastingly discontented with everything... so that you really begin to think, to discover." Unless there is this profound discontent, which is not merely a superficial complaining attitude, there can be no "initiative" and "creativeness." "You have initiative," Krishnamurti explains, "when you initiate or start without being prompted" (39). And this "initiative... becomes creative as it matures; and that is the only way to find out what is truth" (40). Meditative thinking and discontent, thus, are the essence of a meditative curriculum.

Imagining or what Macdonald has also called "mythopoetic imagination" elsewhere ([1981b] 1995), is to balance the dominance of *verbalization*—constant externalizing of meaning, of coming to name the object, and manipulate external reality—in the educational process. Imagining aims to provide an internal referent for the external world. The practical method of mythopoetic imagination is similar to Polanyi's (1967) "indwelling" and what George Steiner (1978) credits Heidegger's life work to be—a process of "radical astonishment." Drawing upon the works of Rudolf Steiner (1968) and the Waldorf Schools, Macdonald thinks that imagination—the ability to picture in the mind what is not present to the senses—is a perceptual power that involves the whole person and puts him or her in contact with the ground of his or her being.[12]

Those who espouse the *Aesthetic principle* (Read 1956) intend to educate children by engaging them in artistic activities. Aesthetic education should help students to move from feeling to drama, sensation to visual and plastic design, intuition to dance and music, and thought to craft. Since aesthetic education—the activities of dramatization, designing, dancing, playing music, and making crafts—aims at allowing students to express their inner creative potential, it forms a key feature of a meditative curriculum.[13]

Macdonald's emphasis upon *body and biology* is to challenge the overemphasis in education on cognitive-verbal learning, which is a kind of fragmentation that separates us from our biological organism. While there has been a lot of discussion of alienation from one's self in a Marxian or Jungian way, alienation from one's body—that may be due to psychological, environmental, and psycho-environmental reasons—is hardly emphasized in educational literature. Understanding one's body and its functions is not merely physical or medical in nature. Understanding one's body and its functions means being aware of its internal as well as external, technical as well as creative, and mundane as well as spiritual dimensions. Having an awareness of one's body is basically a way to be at home—body is our home—to allow centering to happen at a deeper level.

Body is our home and *ecology* is the home for the body. As centering points to unity of the inner being, ecology as a concept emphasizes the unity of life. Therefore, along with educating children to be aware and centered—not self-centered—it is crucial that educational experience also helps children understand how our technological and developmental expansion impacts our planet. It is for the sake of the survival of life on the planet as well as to have a sense of wholeness of being that we need to educate our children and ourselves to be sensitive to the environment and the connection between the inner and the outer.

Learning to be playful, imaginative, meditative (of thoughts, emotions, and body), and artful is in the service of being more perceptive. These are the ways that lead to what Macdonald calls *education for perception* that may open us to many other worlds of consciousness. While Macdonald's proposal regarding education for perception is very important, it would, perhaps, not be possible to actualize his concerns without incorporating awareness or meditative inquiry into the educational process. In the previous chapter, I have shared my understanding of Krishnamurti's insights into awareness or meditative inquiry. Now, I discuss the importance of the art of awareness in relation to the process of education.

Awareness or meditation is "one of the greatest arts in life—perhaps the greatest"; it is an art because "one cannot possibly learn it from another" (Krishnamurti 2002, 2) and it is greatest, for it opens doors to understanding oneself and one's relationship to the whole of life.

The art of awareness subsumes as well as enlivens arts of listening, observation or seeing, dialogue, and learning. The first significant consideration in developing awareness is to give careful attention to one's body, thoughts, and emotions, moment to moment. This observation or careful attention has also to be extended to other people, things, and nature. Second, the art of observation needs to be combined with the art of listening. The art of listening demands an astute listening to oneself, to other people one is engaged with, and also to the sounds of the environment. It is only for the sake of easy comprehension that in his writings Krishnamurti often talks of the listening and observation separately. In actuality, these two become *one* in the act of total attention or meditation, which provides deeper perception into the way life functions. Krishnamurti elaborates (1999b, 57) to children in his school at Rajghat:

[I]f you know how to observe and listen—observing and listening are essentially the same thing, it is all one act—you will find that you take in everything, and are, therefore, immediately aware of everything around you. That will naturally make you highly sensitive; you will be tremendously awake, and your body, your whole being, will come alive.

Also,

If you know how to watch, you will not have to read all the compli-cated books on philosophy or religion. *If you know how to look, how to listen, and how to speak, you will realize that it is all there in your eyes, your ears, and on your tongue.* (56; emphasis added)

Significantly, it is essential for profound listening and observation that they happen without any form of interpretation, judgment, con-demnation, or appreciation. The moment thought interferes with the act of listening and observation there comes a psychological barrier between oneself and others and phenomena, which obstructs intel-ligent perception into the nature of things. In other words, for such observation and listening—the core of meditation or awareness—it is essential that we give our full attention to "what is." "If you ... [listen and observe] ... to have confirmation, to be encouraged in your own thinking, then your listening [and observation] has very little mean-ing. But, if you are listening [and observing] to find out, then your mind is free, not committed to anything; it is very acute, sharp, alive, inquiring, curious, and therefore capable of discovery" (Krishnamurti 1964, 32). Furthermore, when listening and observation happens "with ease, without strain," Krishnamurti explains to children, "you will find an extraordinary change taking place within you, a change which comes about without your volition, without your asking; and in that change there is great beauty and depth of insight" (32).

These two arts—listening and observation—when functioning together bring about a meditative state of mind whereby the other two arts, the arts of dialogue and learning, can flower. Dialogue or conversation defines human relationships. We could not possibly imagine any human system or relationship including education in the absence of communicative action. Yet, we see that it is the communi-cation with each other that has perhaps come to be a real challenge, as also aptly described by the key phrase of curriculum theory, "com-plicated conversation" (Pinar 2012). It is the absence of pure observa-tion and attentive listening that brings about the relational problems, personally and socially. In the absence of clear observation and careful listening, what we see and hear is our own projections about the people and things, based on our conditionings, fears, desires, likes, pursuits, which inhibit a real relationship. *For dialogue, communion, conversation or deeper relationship to happen in schools or in other life situations, it is essential that there be meditative listening and observation.*

The arts of listening, observation, and dialogue form the core of the "art of learning." Learning is not merely accumulation of knowledge from the books. While there is no dispute about the importance of acquiring disciplinary knowledge, the highest function of education, in my view, should be to bring about learning of one's self, which is possible when both teachers and students learn the arts of listening, observation, and dialogue, and which in turn awaken the intelligence among them to make use of the available knowledge rather than being bogged down with it. Therefore, one of the prime functions of right education should be "to give the student abundant knowledge in the various fields of human endeavor and at the same time to free his [her] mind from all tradition [beliefs, superstitions, ideologies, and other conditioning influences] so that he [she] is able to investigate, to find out, to discover" (Krishnamurti 1964, 143). It is only when the mind is free from the burden of knowledge that it can find out about itself. Obviously, in the process of finding out, there should be no accumulation, for accumulation will burden the mind to meet reality—inner and outer—afresh. Krishnamurti elaborates,

> The moment you begin to accumulate what you have experienced or learnt, it becomes an anchorage which holds your mind and prevents it from going further. In the process of [self] inquiry the mind sheds from day to day what it has learnt so that it is always fresh, uncontaminated by yesterday's experience. *Truth is living, it is not static, and the mind that would discover truth must also be living, not burdened with knowledge or experience.* (161; emphasis added)

Indeed, Krishnamurti's exposition regarding awareness provides in-depth and extensive support to Macdonald's concern for centering and transcendence. Now, I turn to discuss the role of the teacher in a pedagogy focused on cultivating awareness and centering.

Unlike transmission and child-centered pedagogic approaches where a teacher is a nonsubjective being and facilitator respectively, "centering" and "meditation" are as critical and significant for the teachers as they are for the students. A teacher who is engaged in the process of centering—of his own and his students—is not judgmental about the students. To understand a child, the teacher should watch her at play, study her in her different moods, but without forming any judgments. The constant judgment on a teacher's part, according to his or her personal likes and dislikes, is bound to create barriers and hindrances in his or her relationship with the child. The beginning of a real relationship between the teacher and the learner starts when the former gives his or her heart to understand the nature of relationship and its complexities of domination, possession, and control. *Right relationship, which comes about through understanding self and its processes, is the beginning of right education.*

A curriculum that supports meditative inquiry, unlike positivist and cognitive approaches, emphasizes *understanding* in the mutually responsive process of centering that involves both students and teachers. In Macdonald's ([1974] 1995) perception,

> Teachers cannot be said to understand children simply because they possess a considerable amount of explicit knowledge about them. *Understanding is a deeper concept.* It demands a sort of indwelling in the other, a touching of the source of the other. Understanding others is not a "useful" procedure in the sense that knowing is...it does not provide the basis for planning, manipulating, and calculating. *Understanding provides the ground for relating, for being fully there in the presence and as a presence to other.* (95; emphasis added)

In other words, understanding is the way to relate at a level much deeper than conditioning—collective and individual. Knowledge of the subject matter and developmental stage of the child may be helpful from a utilitarian educational viewpoint, but a deeper communion between student and teacher requires relating to each other's centers or beings. Macdonald ([1974] 1995) explains further:

> [Understanding] is the process of locating one's center in relation to the other: to "see" one's self and the other in relation to our centers of being; to touch and be touched by another in terms of something fundamental to our shared existence.
>
> This act of relationship, called understanding, ... is an act of listening, but not to the explicit content that a person is expressing. Rather,

it is "tuning in" to the "vibrations" of bodily rhythms, feeling tone, inward expressions of a person's to integrate and to maintain his integrity as a whole person. (95)

Exactly like Krishnamurti, Macdonald ([1974] 1995, 95) also thinks that dialogue or relationship happens when there is the "intent of listening, and listening beneath the surface." Macdonald resonates Krishnamurti's concerns again, when he says that unless there is dialogue, "even the expressions of ideas, of philosophical and religious truths, of psychological insights, is often in the service of the cognitive ego of the participant" (95). *Without listening, there is no dialogue. Without dialogue, there is no relating or understanding. Without understanding, there is no learning. Without learning, there is no living.*

Is what Macdonald calls centering or what Krishnamurti calls awareness self-centered or isolating in nature? What relationship do self-knowledge and self-transformation have with the issues of social change?

SELF-KNOWLEDGE AND SOCIAL CHANGE

Meditative inquiry and the processes of centering and art of awareness, which facilitate the former and, in turn, self-understanding and self-transformation, are certainly self-oriented but not self-centered in nature. Being centered—not self-centered—in one's being or having an awareness of one's self is neither an isolating nor an isolated activity. We do not exist in isolation. We are inherently related to one another because we share human consciousness. *Becoming aware of one's self, indeed, is also a process of becoming sensitive to one's relationship to people, society, and nature.*

In my view, self-transformation is intrinsically related to social transformation. Many people think, especially those who believe in structural transformation, that self-transformation has very little or no effect on society. I object to this understanding. In my view, it is the self and its interactions that form society, and unless the fundamental unit—self—transforms there is no possibility of a profound social change. The change that precedes change in one's consciousness is mechanical, authoritarian, and even totalitarian in nature.

In my understanding, even in a situation when one encloses oneself in a room, one certainly has an effect, however subtle, on the (collective) human consciousness. By separating one's body one cannot separate oneself (individual consciousness) from the consciousness that one shares with the rest of humankind. One may singularize, reconstruct, or restructure that consciousness according to one's way of living, but basically one shares the same consciousness as anybody else on the face of the earth. *So, one's efforts at understanding and transforming oneself, very subtly, influence the whole of consciousness, as the larger movement of consciousness influences oneself.* While changes at the level of the structures are apparent, changes at the level of consciousness are very subtle, but very crucial. "As a physicist," David Bohm says, "I only know that 99 percent of all phenomena occurring in matter and energy are invisible" (Vas 2004, 47). If structures are crystallized forms of our consciousness, then changes in our consciousness, directly or indirectly, also transform our social structures. Indeed, Macdonald argues in his canonical essay, "Curriculum, Consciousness, and Social Change",

> [C]hange in human…consciousness is necessary and [a] precondition of a later political change.…If we utilize the concept of a dialectical relationship over longer periods of time between consciousness and structural change, it is at the "moment" of consciousness in this dialectic whereby we may expect to have any meaningful input in the change process. ([1981a] 1995, 157)

Moreover,

> The work of Gramsci…clearly suggests that liberating social change by necessity involves the breaking up of conditioned and pre-set attitudes, values, and meanings attached to present social phenomena in a manner that allows the person to sense the potential within themselves for change and growth, from powerlessness to power, and from alienation toward relationship and commitment. (163)

This consciousness-oriented perspective helps us realize how critically significant it is for us to understand and transform our consciousness at all levels and in all spheres—individual as well as social. Besides, considering how invisibly and subtly consciousness may influence each and every thing we do—individually or collectively—it is very critical that we do not consider individual and collective consciousness as totally distinct spheres. *Superficially, certainly individual consciousness and collective consciousness seem distinct, but deeply, our consciousness, like our universe, does not have any divisions.*

This point that any fundamental change in social structures is only possible via profound transformation of human consciousness brings Krishnamurti and Macdonald closest to each other in their understanding. Macdonald ([1981a] 1995, 153) asks of us, the educators: Is there anything we can do at the level of schooling that doesn't necessitate prior or concomitant broad social change before it can happen in any meaningful way? Can schools change the social order? These questions certainly represent Krishnamurti's concern regarding the relationship between education and social change too.

Both Macdonald and Krishnamurti give enormous importance to understanding and transforming consciousness in the service of bringing about social transformation. And notably, both of them believe that education is a way to bring about changes in human consciousness and, thereby, in the wider society. It is this conviction for the personal and social transformation that Krishnamurti established schools and study centers in different parts of the world. It is also this stance that pervades Macdonald's profound work. According to Macdonald ([1981a] 1995, 169–170),

> Consciousness is an essential entity of human beings... [it is necessary that we strive] for a basic change in attitudes, values, morals, and perspectives, as well as change in social and economic structure. We in our roles as curriculum teachers and workers can only expect to have influence in the realm of consciousness. This is both a necessary and significant contribution.

Thus, while changes in the structures are important they must begin at the level of consciousness and, as educators, our energies should be directed in understanding how we can perceive and transform our consciousness and the consciousness of people involved in "school in the context of their concrete lived experiences" (157). A change is critical in "consciousness of persons how they 'see' the meaning in the activity they engage in with students and colleagues... [because it] is not enough simply to change the structures or provide new techniques without new lenses of perception and conception" (158–159). In what ways can we bring about change in consciousness? By means of viewing curriculum as meditative inquiry, as I proposed in this chapter.

CONCLUSION

In this chapter, I discussed the essential elements of a meditative curriculum: openness, personal responsiveness, freedom, aesthetics, love, playfulness, meditative thinking, imagining, transcendence, centering, awareness, listening, seeing, and dialogue. Undoubtedly, understanding curriculum as a space of meditative inquiry requires that consciousness and its study and transformation become the core of educational experience. Macdonald's and Krishnamurti's life works provide us with profound insights into the nature of education and invite us to engage and experiment with their perceptions—in our thinking and practice—to find out for our own selves if we can deeply understand and transform our psychological nature and thereby society.

CONCLUSION

> Theoretical prescription or philosophical principles in educa-
> tion are essentially humanistic expressive symbols. They are not
> intended to be (or should not be) taken as literal statements and
> directly translated into action in the same way an experimental
> finding is intended to be used. They are essentially art forms which
> may bring some perspective and may create personal meaning
> within the persons who practice. It is only further witness to the
> contemporary power of culture of science and technology that we
> should expect the same kind of results from them.[1]
>
> —James Macdonald ([1971b] 1995, 57)

INSPIRED BY MACDONALD'S INSIGHTS INTO THE MEANING and significance of theoretical research encapsulated in this beautiful quote,
I would like to describe *Curriculum as Meditative Inquiry* as an "art
form," a "humanistic expressive symbol" that may help us, the educators, to reimagine the whole phenomena of education in a new light
wherein the understanding of consciousness and its transformation
form the core of the educational experience.

While there are definite implications of this work for the discipline
of education, it is not my intention nor is it possible to directly "implement" this work in ways most "experimental" research in education are
conducted and implemented. Its main purpose is to initiate a "complicated conversation," which I think I have accomplished to some
extent in this book, around the points of creative tension—thinking
and analysis vis-à-vis meditative inquiry, subjectivity-as-self vis-à-vis
subjectivity-as-awareness, self-reflexivity vis-à-vis self-awareness,
structure vis-à-vis consciousnesses, and political revolution vis-à-vis
psychological revolution—that I engaged with in my intellectual journey to emphasize the significance of looking at human conflicts and
problems and the ways to approach them from a radically different

perspective. This volume affirms the existence of consciousness and its relationship to the disorder that human beings have created over the earth and calls for a deeper inquiry into one's consciousness and the possibilities of its transformation.

By means of this work, I have investigated the profound relationship among consciousness, meditative inquiry, and curriculum that I have identified in the works of Krishnamurti and Macdonald. Specifically, in this book I engaged with the three central questions:

> *In what ways do the characteristic features of human consciousness—fear, conditioning, becoming, and fragmentation—undermine self-awareness in educational experience?*
>
> *What is meditative inquiry, and how can it help in cultivating awareness, which, in turn, can help in the understanding and transformation of human consciousness?*
>
> *In what ways can we reimagine curriculum as a space for meditative inquiry that may provide self-transformative educational experiences to teachers and their students?*

To fully engage with the first question required an elaborate discussion of the nature of *human consciousness* and the ways in which the former affects and is affected by the character of contemporary educational institutions. Based on my study of the philosophical writings of Krishnamurti, I identified four distinct, yet interrelated, features—fear, conditioning, becoming, and fragmentation—that characterize human consciousness and have their bearing on individual and social conflicts. Then, based on my study of the educational writings of Krishnamurti and the curriculum theory of Macdonald, I identified and explained the ways in which these four features of consciousness shape the nature of contemporary educational institutions. Here I summarize the main arguments.

Fear is, no doubt, a significant aspect of our beings. It would be hard for any of us to deny that fear controls, explicitly or subtly, a great deal of our thoughts, feelings, and actions. Basically, fear is rooted in psychological insecurity and uncertainty. While it would be unrealistic to deny all fears, it is significant to probe the ways in which the search for psychological security and certainty has caused tremendous problems at the personal as well as the social level. It is deep psychological fear and insecurity that is responsible, in many ways, for widespread

inequalities, racial, national, and religious conflicts, as well as discriminations of various sorts. It is in tne search for security—psychological,
not biological—that people accumulate material wealth beyond their
needs. It is also in the search for certainty that people identify themselves
with bigger organizations such as religious groups and nation-states,
which more often than not are created in opposition to other groups
(Krishnamurti [1979] 2005).

Fear certainly plays a very important part in the functioning of
our educational institutions. It is due to the exercise of authority, the
imposition of discipline, and the demand for conformity that schools
cultivate and sustain fear. The school system is usually organized in
a hierarchical system. Students are led by teachers, teachers are led
by administrators, and the latter by district administrators, and the
chain continues. What is the thread that links this chain? Fear of
authority. And to maintain conformity to the authority, there are
disciplinary measures focused on the behaviorist principles of reward
and punishment. In many ways, our schools display autocratic and
military-industrial orientation and function as "total institutions"
(Goffman 1961, xv) such as prisons and mental asylums (Krishnamurti
1953; Macdonald [1971a] 1995).

Conditioning is another very significant factor that cripples our
capacities of "personal responsiveness" (Macdonald [1964] 1995, 17).
Conditioning implies incessant repetition of certain values, beliefs,
and attitudes that shape the way we perceive the world. Certainly, the
selves that we have, and one can see within one's own, is the result
of innumerable conditioning influences: biological, social, historical,
economic, political, and educational. These conditioning influences
have many implications: first, conditioned selves provide conditioned
perceptions of one's own self as well as that of others; second, due to
various sources of conditioning, which are often contradictory, our
selves are divided into different fragments that are generally in conflict with one another. For example, sexuality is a part of the biological conditioning, and religious teachings preach chastity. These
two divergent fragments bring about psychological conflicts. There
could be many other examples particular to our own life histories.
These conditioning influences not only breed conflicts within our
own selves but also between and among us. Undoubtedly, ideological,
religious, nationalistic, and racial divisions could be attributed to various kinds of conditioning influences, which divide people from one

another (Krishnamurti 1970). Education has certainly functioned as a major conditioning tool at the hands of nation-states and organized religions. In addition to the general ethos of schooling, history and civics education have played crucial roles in cultivating nationalistic identities, which are more often than not in conflict with one another (Krishnamurti 1953; K. Kumar 2001, 2007; Lall and Vickers 2009).

The psychological process of *becoming* is yet another factor that negatively influences the quality of awareness. Becoming implies a psychological movement from "what is" to "what should be," which involves psychological time. In the material world the movement from "what is" to "what should" be, for example, the refinement of ores into metal, is a valid process that involves thinking and chronological time. But, the desire to bring about change in the psychological sphere, for example, from fear to non-fear, through the application of thinking and analysis is problematic. In the psychological sphere *the observer is the observed*: the part of the thought that is fearful and the part that wants a state of non-fear are basically two aspects of the same movement. This psychological process of becoming—the observer trying to control and modify the observed—is a separative process of thought that inevitably leads to suppression, conflict, and a waste of energy (Krishnamurti and Bohm 1985).

Becoming in the context of education can be understood in terms of two constructs: ambitions and ideals. Most certainly, our educational institutions implant a cancer of ambition or what Macdonald calls an "ideology of achievement" ([1971b] 1995, 51) in the innocent psyche of children instead of a love of learning. We hardly encourage children to look within themselves and follow their own hearts. Instead, we decide for them, directly or indirectly, personally or socially, what will bring them more success and security. This search for security and success in something other than what one is deeply interested in or capable of is the process of becoming; it is a process of being alienated from one's innermost recess. Ideals in their simplest sense imply something opposite to what actually exists. For example, the ideal of nonviolence exists in opposition to the fact of violence. While it seems absolutely perfect to have ideals, in actuality ideals are very destructive as far as self-understating is concerned. The emphasis on ideals implies that we encourage suppression and condemnation of the actuality—for example, violence—instead of giving our hearts and minds to understanding the fact of violence. Emphasis on ideals rather than facts is a kind of becoming that produces inward conflicts and outward hypocrisy (Krishnamurti 1953, 1964).

Fear, conditioning, and becoming are responsible for individual and social *fragmentation* and conflict. Fragmentation means a state of affairs where different parts—within an individual and in society—are in mutual discord, which inevitably leads to conflict and degeneration. Fear is a tremendous factor of fragmentation. It is due to fear and a deep sense of insecurity—which brings about accumulation, nationalistic and religious divisions, and discriminations of all sorts—that there exists widespread fragmentation. Conditioning influences fuel fragmentation and conflicts within and between individuals and groups. Finally, the process of psychological becoming or time is another form of fragmentation between the "the observer and the observed," leading to psychological conflict and dissipation of energy (Bohm 1980; Krishnamurti [1979] 2005).

In what ways do educational institutions contribute toward fragmentation within individuals and society? First of all, educational institutions cultivate fear by means of imposing authority and discipline and encouraging conformity. Certainly, fear is responsible for suppressing those dimensions of children's beings, which are not in consonance with the respected norms. This suppression results in conflict or fragmentation within children as well as between children and their parents and teachers. Second, contemporary educational institutions encourage "becoming" through emphasizing ambitions and ideals, which divorce children from their innermost beings and bring about alienation. Additionally, conditioning influences from school, state, family, religion, and media create opposing fragments in children's beings that cause conflicts at various levels. Finally, the overemphasis on cognitive aspects at the expense of emotional, bodily, aesthetic, and spiritual dimensions of children's beings is further responsible for fragmentation, which in turn is responsible for their lopsided growth and development (Krishnamurti 1953, 1964; Macdonald [1975c] 1995; Robinson 2001, 2009).

If we acknowledge that our consciousness—the very basis of our thoughts, feelings, and actions—is in conflict and therefore its crystallization or materialization in any form, including in the domain of education, is bound to be conflict-ridden, we need to seriously think about the ways and means to understand the nature of our consciousness and transform it. Krishnamurti's work, which clearly underscores the importance of meditative inquiry in understanding and transforming the nature of consciousness, again proves immensely clarifying. This brings me to my second question: *What is meditative inquiry, and how can it help in cultivating awareness, which, in turn, can help in the understanding and transformation of consciousness?*

Meditative inquiry is an existential process of cultivating an awareness of or becoming attentive to the way one thinks, feels, and acts inwardly as well as in one's relationship to people and nature. Awareness implies a meditative state of mind wherein one listens to and observes people and nature without any interference from the constant movement of thought. Such a meditative listening and observation allows for a deeper perception, communication, and learning, which are transformative in nature. Since meditative inquiry is existential in nature, it stands as a unique and viable approach to addressing conflicts of our consciousness. Why? Because the very nature of our consciousness demands meditative inquiry. Our consciousness is an existential phenomenon, is constantly changing, is in flux, and therefore it cannot be understood and transformed entirely on the basis of theoretical/intellectual/philosophical approaches. The latter use thinking, analysis, system, and authority as their foundations, which are based on thought, which in turn is based on memory and hence past. Thought, which is past, is unable to meet existential problems, such as fear, which is always in the present. Meditative inquiry implies an awareness of the movement of consciousness without any analysis or judgment so that the former may reveal its conflict and be free of it.

Since the conflicts of our consciousness are reflected in the domain of education, which in turn perpetuates the conflicts further, it is important to inquire whether our education helps children and teachers to understand how fear, conditioning influences, becoming, and fragmentation control their thoughts, feelings, and actions. In other words, is there a place for meditative inquiry in most of our educational institutions? Given that most of our contemporary educational institutions are primarily occupied with serving the vested interests of society, it seems highly unlikely that they have any serious considerations to providing opportunities to teachers and their students to inquire, teach, and learn meditatively and thereby understand and transform their consciousness. Recognizing the lack of emphasis on meditative inquiry in educational experience, I argue that a primary function of education should be to provide opportunities for teachers and students so that they may study their consciousness. This brings me to my final question: *In what ways can we reimagine curriculum as a space for meditative inquiry that may provide self-transformative educational experiences to teachers and their students?*

Drawing upon the educational insights of Krishnamurti and Macdonald, I propose viewing curriculum as meditative inquiry. I suggest that meditative study of consciousness—its understanding and transformation—should become the core of educational experience. Curriculum as meditative inquiry emphasizes the significance of the art of awareness and the process of centering in order to have a deeper perception into one's own consciousness and one's relationships. Through incorporating the arts of listening, seeing, and dialogue in the educational experience, curriculum as meditative inquiry aspires to undermine and possibly dissolve the factors of fear, conditioning, becoming, and fragmentation to bring about integrated human beings. Curriculum as meditative inquiry also encourages the cultivation of the qualities of openness, aesthetics, and freedom in educational process for optimum actualization of students' and their teachers' inner potential. Viewed from the perspective of meditative inquiry, education no more remains a problem of information transmission or means-end learning or performance on standardized tests. On the contrary, with meditative inquiry as its guiding principle, education emerges as a space of freedom where the main focus is to learn about oneself and one's relationships to people, nature, and ideas.

CONTRIBUTIONS TO EDUCATIONAL
THEORY AND PEDAGOGY

First of all, this work sheds light on the ongoing debates that are concerned with understanding which of the two—structure or consciousness—is the key element in the process of transformation. Due to the structuralist and poststructuralist attack on the subject in education (Pinar 2009b), on the one hand, and the under consideration of the works of individuals such as Krishnamurti, Gurdjieff, Osho, and Bohm, on the other hand, I think my expositions regarding the extraordinary importance of understanding and transforming consciousness is an important contribution to educational theory. While there is no denial to the importance of structures, I think it is the path of deeply considering the nature of our consciousness that has much greater promise than relying on structural change alone. Depending on structural change, which becomes static once carried out, is dangerous; for, there is the possibility that structures become mechanical, even totalitarian and authoritarian, if looked at as something devoid of any connections with consciousness, which has actually brought them into existence in the first place.

The next contribution of this research is to affirm consciousness and its study and transformation as a central dimension of educational experience. Significantly, studying one's consciousness, which intrinsically is also the consciousness of humankind, is not collecting discrete information about one's mind, body, and feelings, nor is it self-criticism or self-reflection, although these all have their value and place in learning and living. Self-knowing—the study of one's consciousness—is more like a verb rather than a noun. It is a never-ending search of one's existence and one's relationship to people and nature through meditative awareness. Bringing consciousness to the centre of the study of educational experience is a major contribution to expanding the horizons of educational theory.

Additionally, my work suggests the significance of understanding how human consciousness and education are profoundly connected with each other. That is, if we want to understand the phenomenon of education, we cannot avoid probing how human consciousness crystallizes itself in the domain of education: in the form of defining goals of education, delineating the rules of behavior, ascertaining the roles of teachers and students, establishing the nature of relationships among people involved, and determining the nature of subject matter, pedagogic practices, and evaluation procedures. It is my contention that unless we give our sustained attention to the psychological connections of educational processes, there is a strong likelihood that the latter will continue to perpetuate the conflicted nature of our consciousness. This is a unique contribution to educational theory for few have considered the problem of consciousness and education together in such a detailed manner.

My explications of the meaning and significance of the notion of "awareness" from four distinct points of view is also an important contribution to educational theory. There are three established viewpoints that invoke different meanings of what it means to be "aware": information transmission, social criticism, and self-reflection. As I have explained previously, the way I view it, "awareness" or meditative inquiry is not equivalent to accumulating information, criticizing social reality, or being self-reflexive. While all the preceding associations with the term "awareness" are significant in their own right and should be part of the educational experience, it is the meditative connotation of awareness and its significance to the educational experience that this book is primarily about.

Laying the foundations of understanding curriculum as meditative inquiry constitutes another significant contribution to educational theory as well as to pedagogy. Based on my engagements with the ideas of Krishnamurti and Macdonald, I have identified and theorized the basic elements of a meditative curriculum—personal responsiveness, openness, freedom, creativity, meditative thinking, playfulness, centering, and awareness—that I believe have the potential for providing self-transformative opportunities for students and teachers. My attempt at bringing Krishnamurti and Macdonald together is another contribution, for up until now nobody has associated their works together.[2] As is explicit from this volume, their works resonate with each other remarkably and provide a strong foundation for reimagining curriculum as a space for self-transformative teaching and learning.

While there exists examples of studies on Krishnamurti's work in education,[3] this is a first major work in the field of curriculum studies. In this undertaking, I have integrated a large body of Krishnamurti's work in order to systematically articulate the important insights available in his writings. While I have depended upon his insights to a great deal, the organization, articulation, and in many cases, explication of his ideas with relation to social and educational problems constitutes my original contribution. This is also the first major study that incorporates Macdonald's work to such an extent in curriculum theory. I hope this research incites new interest in Macdonald's important work, which is unfinished and can be developed in many directions.[4]

LIMITATIONS OF THE VOLUME

Curriculum as Meditative Inquiry is a philosophical work. It does not incorporate any empirical data or conduct any policy analysis. It primarily aims at theoretical engagement with the issues that in my view should be at the heart of educational theory and pedagogy: human consciousness, meditative inquiry, and curriculum, and their intricate relationships with one another. Its purpose is not to provide any "experimental findings" to "fix" educational institutions through "curriculum development" and "reform." On the contrary, it is primarily concerned with provoking thinking regarding the fundamental questions: In what ways are our consciousness and education related? How can we view educational experience as meditative inquiry into the depth of our beings?

Although my work alludes to the impacts of standardization and market forces in reducing education to the level of a commodity, most of my discussion does not consider any specific context, for example, the nightmare of neoliberal education reforms (Ross and Gibson 2007). School "reform," beyond doubt, presents tremendous challenges for anybody—teachers, students, parents, and administrators—who aspire to understand and practice the "philosophical principles" (Macdonald [1971] 1995, 57) that underlie curriculum as meditative inquiry.

While I did briefly discuss the Marxist and psychoanalytic conceptualizations of consciousness, my discussion of the nature of consciousness is primarily based on the study of Krishnamurti's work. Moreover, like consciousness, meditative inquiry is also a vast field. There exist numerous perspectives—new and old—on what it means to inquire into one's consciousness to understand and transform the latter. Krishnamurti holds a radically different perception on the nature of meditation. It is primarily to keep the distinctness of Krishnamurti's vision and his profound insights that I decided not to include other approaches to meditative inquiry in my discussion.

SUGGESTIONS FOR FUTURE INQUIRY

The central proposal of this book—curriculum as meditative inquiry—can be extended in several directions. I believe that a careful study of the works of Gurdjieff, Bohm, and Osho, with a particular focus on self-remembering and self-observation (Ouspensky 1949), thought as a system (Bohm 1992), wholeness and the implicate order (Bohm 1980), dialogue (Bohm 1996), creativity (Bohm 1998), and meditative therapies (Osho 1996), should enable interested educators, including myself, to further explore the possibilities of expanding, deepening, and enriching the idea of a meditative curriculum.

Moreover, there exist possibilities to extend research on the points of tension between meditative inquiry and critical pedagogy with

reference to the problems of structure and consciousness and psychological and political change, as I explored to some extent in this volume. Also, research possibilities exist with regard to understanding
the relationship between currere and meditation. Research could also
be conducted to understand the significance of a meditative inquiry
for the area of holistic education.

There are several possibilities for intriguing studies of Krishnamurti's
significance for curriculum theory: Krishnamurti's and Dewey's idea
of intelligence, experience, and truth; Krishnamurti's idea of awareness
and Freire's idea of critical consciousness; Krishnamurti's and Marxist
and neo-Marxist ideas of revolution; Krishnamurti's and Deleuze's
concepts of fragmentation and time; Krishnamurti and psychoanalysis; Krishnamurti and phenomenology; Krishnamurti and existentialism; Krishnamurti and postmodernism, with special reference to his
concept of conditioning and Foucault's concepts of regimes of truth
and processes of normalization, Derrida's ideas of discourse and text,
and Deleuze's idea of territorialization, among others. Finally, since
Krishnamurti has also established several educational institutions,
there are possibilities to conduct empirical research to study the field
dynamic of his insights in the life world of the school.[5]

Macdonald's work has not received much attention in spite of its
significant potential for educational theory and pedagogy. There are
several possibilities for exploring Macdonald's work further. His initial theorization of invaluable concepts needs to be expanded and
enriched. Some of the concepts that I really consider worth exploring, as I have also tried in this book and will do so in future, include
openness, personal responsiveness, reality-centered schools, aesthetics,
mythopoetic imagination, playfulness, meditative thinking, centering, transcendence, understanding, listening, education for perception, and freedom, among others. Moreover, one may also conduct
empirical studies to understand the significance of suggestions offered
in Macdonald's work—for example, playfulness and meditative
thinking—in classroom situations. There is also the possibility of
comparing Macdonald's works with other curriculum theorists, for
example, his friend and colleague Dwayne Huebner.

I conclude with the hope that the readers of *Curriculum as
Meditative Inquiry* will share their criticisms, comments, and questions to help me advance the "complicated conversation" that I have
attempted to initiate by means of this work.

AFTERWORD

WHEN ASHWANI KUMAR FIRST CAME TO MY OFFICE INQUIRING INTO my interest in Jiddu Krishnamurti, I was surprised, but pleasantly so. Educational research rarely cites Krishnamurti's work; you would not generally find the nature of his questions and themes explicitly raised in a scholarship examining curriculum. I have, however, published an article in a curriculum journal and two chapters in edited books relevant to teaching that refer to Krishnamurti's work. My interest in his dialogues relates to my teaching of a course I had developed, called Living Inquiry, which studies awareness and attention in daily living. Krishnamurti's lifework has provided me with an "existential approach" toward understanding "being" in everyday life, as have several Eastern and Western philosophers and phenomenologists.

In *Curriculum as Meditative Inquiry*, Ashwani argues that meditative inquiry is such an existential approach "to comprehend and transform human consciousness," which he claims, as did Krishnamurti, is "in conflict" (this volume, 36). One distinction I would add here is that understanding or comprehending conflict *within* human consciousness through inquiry *is* transformational. For me, this subtle point focuses attention on inquiry as a conscious, living practice in flux (*fluere*, to flow) as is transformation (*trans*, across; *formare*, to form).

Ashwani was a graduate student the day we met, and he listened politely to my rather long story of discovering Krishnamurti's work. I first found *The Awakening of Intelligence* (Krishnamurti 1973) nearly 40 years ago while in my early twenties. The find was a fortunate fluke. Imagine the mid-1970s and a young woman—long skirt, macramé purse, and Rasta-colored scarf—rummaging through a bookstore (the kind with burning incense and tie-dyed curtains) for something to read that would justify or just explain her restlessness about pretty much everything about the world. My public education thus far felt like a complete bust, "stuck inside clichéd textbooks that dodged any scent of controversy" (Cohen et al. 2012, 110). Ashwani maintains, as does James Macdonald, that such avoidance of controversial issues in school curriculum is based on a fear of losing control and constructing effective and orderly activities (this volume, 62). He argues that "discipline instead of intelligence and sensitivity" plays a significant role in such control (this volume, 63). What I do recall as a student was that the curriculum was closed to inquiry and I did not understand why.

So even at my young age, I was struck by Krishnamurti's intense appeal to see the movement of life, the whole of it, "as it is," with open, fresh, inquiring eyes, free from preferences and attachments. He called us "second-hand beings" due to our severe conditioning. *The Awakening of Intelligence* was the first book I ever bought, and I lived between and inside its lines for months, trying to find answers. We did part ways before long, the book and I, both of us lost, me in the Heideggerian sense, lost in the "They" and idle chat of the world.

I bought and read the book several more times in the next three decades (when borrowers never returned it) before my serious study of Krishnamurti's work and my development of curriculum designed to initiate a practice of inquiry into "how we participate in the structure, content, and movement of daily life, how we experience our inner and outer worldliness in everyday living" (Cohen et al. 2012, 111). Krishnamurti called such awareness "intelligence," when the experiencing self is actively conscious of what goes on in everyday life.

Writing this Afterword for *Curriculum as Meditative Inquiry* felt appropriate to me since I aspire to integrate much of what Ashwani argues there, particularly in my articulations of Living Inquiry, which I teach with practicing teachers, graduate students, and several years back with grade seven students. For the Afterword, I chose to reflect on these specific cases and contexts: How does "curriculum as meditative inquiry" *work*?

My most memorable class discussion in Living Inquiry is related to the theme of time (one of four themes in the course: place, language, time, and self/other). I recall the weekly field note a student brought in to share for our collective inquiry, which sparked the intense discussion (students' weekly field notes are meditative inquiries and become content for the course). The field note included an abstract painting that featured an infinity symbol. Our spirited and sophisticated dialogue travelled from the movement of time to the possibilities of beginnings and endings, religion, scientism, mortality, and so on. When I heard a bell ring, signaling the end of class, I suddenly remembered I was in an elementary school rather than the university, among eleven- and twelve-year-olds. I was wholly impressed by their enthusiasm to talk about their experiences and the meanings they ascribe to the existence of time.

Their teacher had taken the Living Inquiry course as a graduate student and asked me to work with her to develop and implement a similar curriculum for her students. I agreed and visited her grade six/seven class once a week for the next two years. The themes we covered (place, language, time, and self/other) and the dialogues that arose were certainly not part of a traditional school curriculum. The students' practices of attending to daily life in their field notes appeared to be no more difficult than what I encounter with graduate students.

As a curriculum, such inquiry opens up what Natasha Levinson (2001) calls teaching in the midst of "belatedness," whereby young people find themselves in a world built and discovered prior to their arrival, finding themselves treated as if they've been here before. Curriculum as meditative inquiry not only examines the world "as it is" but also, I believe, preserves students' capacity to imagine it otherwise, "as a legitimate way of knowing" (Brueggemann 2001, x). That is, such curriculum provides the space for young people to *openly* explore and understand their relationship with the world and "conceivably push back the notion that they are always already determined and fated by it" (Meyer 2010, 88). Levinson's notion of "belatedness" explains my adolescent restlessness and confusion about the world. The challenge for educators is to create pedagogical spaces in which students can understand and confront their sense of belatedness (and social positioning) without feeling paralyzed or determined by it.

In my work with practicing, inner city teachers, our living inquiries focus on what it means to belong in a modern urban world as well as what "cosmopolitan care" (as action) means to education. The intent of meditative inquiry (reflected in weekly field notes related to the four themes) is to develop "a discriminating attunement and immediacy to our urban location and context and the subtleties of its structure" (Meyer 2010, 87). Together the teachers interpret their experiences of urban-ness in everyday life and their teaching practices within the complexities, history, and cultural forms the city offers: "a space of displacement, gatherings, and taking a distance" (Ricoeur 2004, 151).

The fact is that every neighborhood has a school and teachers find themselves and their practice bound to the institution of "public" school, which constitutes a reality that is seen and heard by everyone (Arendt 1958). Public perceptions of teachers arise from influences of culture, media and government policy, alongside a common, commodified view of education, whereby student achievement is a product of teachers' work, students are consumers, and learning is a product created for them not by them (Veto 2012). An unfortunate result, according to Veto, is that "the teacher part of the system is clearly blamed as the cause of poor student achievement" (8). In the course, the teachers' living inquiries offer a counter discourse to this adamant one they are enmeshed in. Inquiring into place (as public space) and language (as a discourse around media, government policy, authority, accountability, etc.) is particularly critical.

In "The Crisis of Education" Arendt (1977) argues that one responsibility of education is to introduce students to the world "as it is," with all its flaws, yet not dictating what we might want it to be. She states, "The teacher's qualifications consist in knowing the world and being able to instruct others about it...pointing out the details and saying to the child: This is our world" (186). A second responsibility relates to action and nurturing the capacity for action, creating "the conditions for what Arendt calls 'setting-right' of the world" (Levinson 2001, 18). Ashwani makes a similar claim:

> The concern of the educator should be to help students understand the complexities of his or her whole being rather than compelling them to suppress one part of their personality for the benefit of some other part; for, suppression inevitably leads to inward and outward conflict. (this volume, 63)

If this is indeed the case, there needs to be space in university for beginning and practicing teachers to explore, as meditative inquiry, their own social and physical realities, common practices, expectations, and the deeper normative notions and imaginaries underlying these expectations (Meyer 2010, 87). Here inquiry is an act that furthers action toward "setting-right of the world." Thus, teaching

Living Inquiry at the university means creating critical, living spaces of inquiry (in Teacher Education, in undergraduate education), rather than more fragmented disciplinary curriculum. Ashwani reminds us that "since our thinking is governed by fragmentary thoughts, whatever we throw our eyes on becomes fragmented" (this volume, 53).

Furthermore, in graduate studies at the university, students are also members of a community of researchers. An approach of meditative inquiry with graduate students means critical attention to "who" they are as researchers, acting inside an institution with particular politics and scholarship that underlie and impact the decisions they will make as researchers. Like all researchers, graduate students will soon find themselves in the position of comparing (seeking to differentiate, hierarchize, homogenize, and exclude), and in the process of doing so, naming what is "normal" and who and what are delinquent (Meyer and Fels 2009, 279). Gadamer reminds us about the consequences on the whole of our civilization founded on modern science and the possibility of remaining half in the dark with what has been omitted and misinterpreted: "cannot the result be that the hand applying this knowledge will be destructive?" (1976, 10).

Will we always remain half in the dark? Can we "set right" what has been omitted and misinterpreted? As Ashwani argues, without a change in consciousness we will inevitably see the world in the same fragmented, conditioned patterns. *Curriculum as Meditative Inquiry,* as a "complicated conversation," reimagines the whole phenomenon of education anew wherein "the understanding of consciousness and its transformation form the core of the educational experience" (this volume, 119). I am grateful for the many complicated conversations Ashwani and I have shared around curriculum and inquiry since he first showed up at my office and politely listened to my stories of learning and teaching. I am also grateful that such a provocative text now exists in educational research and inspires teachers and students to work together and imagine the world other*wise.*

KAREN MEYER
Associate Professor
The University of British Columbia
Vancouver

NOTES

SERIES EDITOR'S INTRODUCTION

1. Quoted in this volume.
2. Quoted in Christian (1996, 358).
3. Grant (1998 [1974], 84).
4. All quoted passages in this paragraph from this volume.
5. Quoted passages in this paragraph from this volume.

INTRODUCTION

1. Relationship between "structures" and "consciousness" vis-à-vis the notion of "transformation" is a central and, hence, recurrent theme all through this book.
2. Given their tremendous contribution to my work as well as due to a general lack of knowledge about their lives and works in education literature, I provide brief biographical introductions about them in the next chapter.
3. Krishnamurti uses several words—for example, meditation, total attention, and pure observation—interchangeably to convey what he means by "awareness."
4. I will discuss in detail the nature of consciousness and its characteristic features (fear, becoming, conditioning, and fragmentation) in chapter 2 and how these influence the nature of contemporary educational institutions in chapter 3.
5. In chapter 5, I will discuss in detail the essential elements of a meditative curriculum.
6. In chapter 4, I will discuss in detail the meaning and significance of "meditative inquiry" in the understanding and transformation of human consciousness.
7. I must clarify here that my criticism of information transmission is not the criticism of information per se. It is, of course, impossible to deny the necessity of information. Information is important, even

essential, to cultivating awareness (Pinar, pers. comm.), provided it is subject to careful deliberation. Focus on information becomes problematic when transmission—which does not problematize the selection, production, and distribution of information and ignores the importance of consciousness—rather than comprehension becomes the goal.

8. Many Marxist and neo-Marxist educators (e.g., McLaren and Kincheloe 2007) think that due to Freire's (1973) theorization of "critical consciousness," they have been able to bring "consciousness" to their materialistic conceptions of education and society. In my view, Freire's notion of "critical consciousness" is still materialistic. According to Freire: "Critical consciousness is the ability to perceive social, political, and economic oppression and to take action against the oppressive elements of society" (1973, 35). Is not Freire's consciousness structure or material centered? He does not even mention the subjective-psychological state of individuals in defining the central concept of his philosophy, let alone delving into the depths and mysteries of consciousness, which is a deep and vast field. Freire's work is more about *consciousness of* rather than *consciousness itself.*

9. As I will briefly explain in my autobiographical reflections in the next chapter, I was also influenced by the critical theory and pedagogy tradition, particularly the work of Paulo Freire, for its focus on critical consciousness, as is explicit in my writings (A. Kumar 2007, 2008a, 2008b, 2008c, 2009, 2012). There is no doubt that critical pedagogy and its proponents have played a major role in understanding the historical, political, and economic character of curriculum and schooling and rightly emphasized the need for revolution. However, as I tried to note in the main text, when looked at more closely, critical pedagogy and its central concern—critical consciousness—are primarily society oriented and do not shed much light upon the psychological roots of our exploitative and oppressive social structures, which, among other things, is one of the main focuses of understanding curriculum as meditative inquiry.

10. Undoubtedly, autobiography represents a revolutionary advancement in the field of education. It has brought back with great force the most important aspect of the educational process: subjectivity. It certainly has given depth to the notion of education by criticizing the behavioristic and positivistic orientations of the curriculum development paradigm, on the one hand, and structural preoccupation of Marxist and neo-Marxist analyses, on the other hand. It is owing to my recognition of the tremendous importance of autobiography that in the next chapter I provide biographical sketches of Krishnamurti

and Macdonald and share some relevant aspects of my own personal history. However, as I have tried to explain in the main text, auto-biography is primarily concerned with reflexive-critical-intellectual engagement with the Ego and its modification; but it does not see the latter as the root of psychological and social problems, which is the main focus of meditative inquiry.

11. I encounter great reactions in academia against spiritual or mystical thoughts and experiences. What are we against: mysticism or what Freire (1973, 102) terms "mythecization"? *Is this not denial, without a real inquiry or search into mystical experiences, if there are any, being positivistic?* Naturally, being positivistic means remaining confined to the surface of our existence, to the observable. Is not thought a mate-rial/observable process? Thought is of course the response of memory, which is stored up in our brains, and thus a material and observable reality, however deeper (individual and collective unconscious) that might be. Thus, without exploring a deeper dimension or the mysti-cal experience, if you will, of one's own subjectivity, is not one inad-vertently developing a positivistic view of reality? I personally do not think that our selves are limited to what we know usually. In other words, there are deeper functions in existence beyond matter (thought too is a material process). However, I do not say that one should believe in the profoundness of existence and one's own self. In the inner world neither theists nor atheists have any value. What is important to find out is whether there are any deeper recesses in ourselves, which we have not touched. Can we live at a deeper level than we are living presently, which is primarily the never-ending movement of thought?

12. While not fully conscious of its implications, my first introduction to the importance of self-understanding was in my high school when I had the opportunity to read the poetry of Kabir (1440–1518)—a fifteenth-century mystic, poet, and philosopher whose revolutionary verses form an important part of Indian literature. Shabana Virmani, a famous documentary filmmaker, produced four remarkable, award-winning documentaries on Kabir in 2008 (These documentaries are available online at: http://www.cultureunplugged.com/documentary/watch-online/festival/gsearch.php#q=Kabir&label=movies). As far as I remember, I was free of the clutches of organized religion very early in my life, and my mother who is the heart—head is too masculine a term—of the family, as my father has been suffering from severe men-tal illness, fortunately never imposed Hindu religion on me.

13. George Gurdjieff (1866–1949) was an extraordinary Russian mystic who contributed immensely to the study of human consciousness. He developed meditative practices, dances, and music to guide the

process of self-transformation. The best introduction to his teachings is *In Search of the Miraculous* (1949), authored by Peter D. Ouspensky, who was a famous philosopher and a disciple of Gurdjieff. In his own writings (1950, 1963, 1975) Gurdjieff's main intention, in my understanding, was not to provide information to the reader; it was to challenge them to be attentive while reading.

14. Osho (1931–1990) was a highly controversial mystic from India who contributed immensely to the science of meditation. Osho's most significant contribution is the development of hundreds of methods of meditation (see, for example, Osho 1996, 1998) by adapting and refining old and existing methods and by creating new ones, keeping in mind the nature of present-day human beings. These methods of meditation, ranging from very active, such as Dynamic and Kundalini, to very passive, such as Vippassna, keep astute observation and awareness, choicelessness, and relaxation at their core. His discourses, which reflect on and deconstruct the religious, mystical, and philosophical traditions of the East and the West and which combine his deep insights in human psychology and the possibilities of the latter's transformation, have been compiled into hundreds of books. I came to know about Krishnamurti and his work from Osho's literature.

15. I would like to especially thank the following colleagues and friends for their engagement with my work: Ahmed Rahim, Ashutosh Kalsi, Evelyn Loewen, Hannah Spector, Joanne Price, John Schellenberg, Lauren Hall, Manasi Thapliyal, Mary Ann Chacko, Michael MacDonald, Mindy Carter, Trudy Bergere, and William Hare, among others.

1   KRISHNAMURTI, MACDONALD, AND MYSELF

1. The Theosophical Society was founded in 1875 in New York by Helana Blavatsky and Henry Steel Olcott. It was created to promote harmony in the world and to study world religions, with a special focus on the religions in India.

2. In the yogic system all of us have a deeper source of energy within us that lies dormant near generative organs unless awakened deliberately. This energy is called Kundalini energy, which moves through the spinal chord toward the brain activating its latent potentials. Krishnamurti had hardly talked about his experiences in public, because he never wanted to portray himself as somebody special. The focus of his whole effort, until he died, was to help people see the conflict in consciousness and inquire whether this conflict can come to an end.

3. The "Order of the Star in the East" was founded in 1911 to proclaim the coming of the "World Teacher." Krishnamurti was appointed as the Head of the Order. On August 2, 1929, on the opening day of the annual Star Camp at Ommen (Holland) Krishnamurti dissolved the Order before three thousand members. The full text of his speech can be accessed online at: http://www.jkrishnamurti.org /about-krishnamurti/dissolution-speech.php.

4. It may be pointed out that education was a key concern for Krishnamurti and directly or indirectly all of Krishnamurti's books have significant implications for the field of education.

5. The author of *Education as Service* (1912), like *At the Feet of the Master* (1910), is listed as "Alcyone." These two books are supposed to have been written by Krishnamurti while he was still being groomed as the upcoming "World Teacher" by the theosophists. While there is considerable controversy regarding the authorship of *At the Feet of the Master*, many people, including Scott H. Forbes (1994), a Portland (Oregon) based holistic educator who worked for 20 years (10 years as Principal) at the Brockwood Park Krishnamurti Educational Centre in England and now is the executive director of the Holistic Education Incorporation, considers that Krishnamurti wrote, at least, parts of *Education as Service*. After 1929, the year when Krishnamurti dissolved the "Order of the Star in the East" and distanced himself from the Theosophical Society, he started giving talks and conducting discussions in different parts of the world to share his insights into the nature and implications of individual and social conflicts. After World War II, on the encouragement of his close friend Aldous Huxley, Krishnamurti also started writing books while continuing to give talks and conduct dialogues. The title of his first authored book—*Education and the Significance of Life*—that he wrote in 1953 shows Krishnamurti's deep concerns on the role and function of education in bringing about a new human being and a new society.

6. The other major educational texts by Krishnamurti include: *Life Ahead: On Learning and the Search for Meaning* (1963); *This Matter of Culture* (also published under the title: *Think on These Things*) (1964); *Talks with American Students* (1968); *You are the World* (1972); *Krishnamurti on Education* (1974); *Beginnings of Learning* (1975); *Inward Flowering* (1976); *A Flame of Learning* (1993); *A Timeless Spring: Krishnamurti at Rajghat* (1999b); *What are You Doing with Your Life?* (2001); and *Krishnamurti for the Young: A Series of Three Books* (Three Volumes) (2004).

7. For further details about Krishnamurti's schools see: http://www.kfa .org/links_schools.php. Krishnamurti's schools also have adjoining

study centers for anybody who is interested in learning and exploring Krishnamurti's work and one's own self. The Oak Grove School in Ojai Valley, California also offers Teaching Academy several times every year which can be attended by anybody who wants to engage with Krishnamurti's educational insights. The University of California, Santa Barbara Extension offers four units of professional-level credit for the Teaching Academy courses. For further details see: http://www.kfa.org/teaching-academy.php.

8. The nature of Krishnamurti's influence varied in terms of how people incorporated his insights into their lives and works. For some, such as David Bohm, Krishnamurti's insights were helpful in understanding the nature of time and space as well as the crisis of human civilization. While many had direct contact with Krishnamurti, there were people such as Henry Miller (1969) who deeply appreciated Krishnamurti and his work from a distance. There are also many intellectuals, for example, Karen Meyer (2006, 2010), who never met Krishnamurti, but are profoundly touched by his perceptions regarding the notions of consciousness and awareness. To know more about the nature of Krishnamurti's influence on many world-renowned people consult Evelyne Blau's *Krishnamurti: 100 Years* (1995).

9. Krishnamurti's address to the UN can be accessed at: http://www.krishnamurtiaustralia.org/articles/world_peace.htm. For a video recording see: http://www.guba.com/watch/3000138398.

10. Krishnamurti's life and works have been subject to extensive research, which include: Principal biographies: Jayakar (1986), Lutyens (1975, 1983, 1988, 1990, 1996); Other Biographies/Memoirs/Reminiscences: Balfour-Clarke (1977), Blau (1995), Blackburn (1996), Chandmal (1985), Field and Hay (1989), Grohe (2001), Holroyd (1991), Krohnen (1996), Lutyens (1957), Narayan, (1999), Nearing (1992), Patwardhan (1999), Ross (2000), Sloss (1991), Smith (1989), and Vernon (2002), among others; Theoretical works: Boutte (2002), Delkhah (1997), Dhopeshwarkar ([1967] 1993), Grego (1997), Han (1991), Heber (1935), Holden (1972), Holroyd (1980), Kalsi (2007), Kobbekaduwa (1990), Khattar (2001), Martin (1975), Martin (2003), Miller (1969), Moffatt (1976), Needleman (1970), Rommelaere (1976), Rodrigues (1990), Sabzevary (2008), Sanat (1999), Suares (1953), Thuruthiyil (1999), and Vas (1971, 2004) among others; Empirical works: Cloninger (2008); Thapan ([1991] 2006); and Documentaries/Films: Govindon (1985) and Mendizza (1984, 1990), among others.

11. For biographical information about Macdonald I primarily depended upon Melva M. Burke's (1985) *JCT* (*Journal of Curriculum*

Theorizing) essay—"The Personal and Professional Journey of James B. Macdonald"—that in turn is derived from her doctoral dissertation (Burke 1983). Burke interviewed Macdonald for many hours from November, 1982, through August, 1983. During this time Macdonald was hospitalized due to a kidney failure and was on a dialysis machine.

12. Macdonald's intellectual journey characterizes four stages, as he himself discussed in a videotaped autobiography (Brubaker and Brookbank 1986): scientific thinking, personal humanism, sociopolitical humanism, and transcendental thought (Burke 1985). "The phases or stages [of Macdonald's work]," as Burke (1985, 116) points out, "do not appear to be mutually exclusive; instead, they represent turns in the road rather than new roads and indicate a meaningful evolution of thought." Macdonald believed that each stage was necessary and important to his study of what he considered the key question in curriculum: How shall we live together (Pinar 1995, 9; also see Brubacker and Brookbank 1986; Macdonald 1986)? Scientific thinking dominated Macdonald's initial intellectual career for almost ten years, which he renounced because of its "dehumanizing" character. His career from the middle of the 1960s onward characterizes his concerns for humanistic, transformative, and transcendental education.

13. This last essay is one of the most influential essays of Macdonald. It is also after reading this essay that I myself decided to read Macdonald's work further. It is significant to point out that Macdonald's view of social change was not structure oriented. In his view, the most significant contribution that we, educators, can make is in the field of consciousness that, in turn, will bring about change in the social structures.

14. Before coming to The University of British Columbia in Vancouver, I spent all my life in New Delhi. I completed my school education from Hindi language government schools (except for three years from grade 6–8 when I studied in a mediocre private school, because my sister taught in that school). Afterward, I completed five degrees— three in Geography and two in Education—from different colleges and departments of the University of Delhi.

15. *Dhyan Sutra* (*Principles of Meditation*) is a small Hindi book of about one hundred and fifty pages that contains seeds for radical inner psychological transformation. It exposits upon the ways one can purify one's body, mind, and emotions through catharsis followed by deep and silent meditation based on the perspicacious observation of the movement of one's thoughts, feelings, and actions. I lived this book

with as much intensity as I could and it provided a strong foundation to my search for self-understanding.

16. It needs to be pointed out that I was not the only student who was dissatisfied with what was going on in the department. Many of my friends in the same program felt the same way about the quality of curriculum and teaching. With the exception of a few courses, I have no hesitation in saying that I learnt much more—as far as the institutional input is concerned—in my undergraduate program when compared with my time in MA and MPhil programs.

17. It was in my seventh or eighth attempt that I finally passed this examination just before leaving New Delhi for Vancouver to pursue my doctoral studies at The University of British Columbia.

18. Anurag and Rajeev have been my fellow travelers on this pathless path of self-inquiry. When I was in New Delhi for about ten years, we discussed, and discussed, and discussed ... daily. We also meditated together, which primarily involved experimenting with Osho's methods and techniques. Our parents and friends were bewildered about what it was that we talked about everyday and how come we became interested in meditation at such an early age. These discussions and meditations have helped me go deeply into understanding my own psychological nature. A great deal of what I say in this book was always present, if in its seed form, in our discussions.

19. I had the privilege to learn from late professor K. K. Mojumdar for over ten years when I was a student at University of Delhi. He was an excellent teacher, who never came to class with any fixed ideas. His spontaneity, creativity, and conviviality always amazed me. He had remarkable insights in geographical thought, politics, religion, philosophy, education, and psychology, each of which helped me to appreciate the importance of looking at things from multiple perspectives. While he absolutely loved to talk, he was also able to listen and was very open. On one occasion when we were talking on the balcony of his university apartment in New Delhi, I remember very distinctly to have said this: "Sir, you do not exactly understand what Krishnamurti and Bohm are saying about 'psychological time' in *The Ending of Time*. You are appropriating their ideas to your own end." He paused for a while and then said this: "Alright, let us study *The Ending of Time* together and help me to see what it is that I am not understanding." How remarkable was he as a teacher. How fortunate was I as a student.

20. *Meetings with Remarkable Men* (Brook 1979) is an excellent movie about the early life of Russian mystic, George Gurdjieff. This movie is based on Gurdjieff's autobiographical book with the same title. Anybody who is interested in understanding the passion, intensity,

and thirst of somebody and who really wants to find out the meaning of life must watch this movie.

21. D. K. Bedi had a fine academic bent. Interestingly, he also liked reading Krishnamurti and Osho. While we never talked at length, he supported me in many ways during my stay at the school and encouraged me to continue my studies.

22. At the CIE (University of Delhi) I was extremely fortunate to have got a chance to meet Professors Rama Mathew and Shyam Menon. Both of them really appreciated my thinking and work and strongly supported me to go abroad for doctoral studies.

23. I had the great opportunity to learn from Professor William F. Pinar since my first day at The University of British Columbia. My doctoral research, which is the basis of this book, would not have been possible had he not accepted me as his student. I have no hesitation in saying that he let me do the work that many might not deem "educational enough." Though Professor Pinar disagreed with me on many points, he never suppressed me from doing the kind of work that I wanted to do. On the contrary, he engaged me in, what he creatively calls, "complicated conversation." It was these conversations we had together which contributed most significantly to my learning experience as a doctoral student. Besides, I received generous funding and learnt a great deal and wrote about the character of curriculum studies in Brazil, Mexico, and South Africa (A. Kumar 2010, 2011a, 2011b) from working as a research assistant on Professor Pinar's internationalization of curriculum studies projects. I truly appreciate Professor Pinar's serious consideration of subjective consciousness in educational experience, passion for intense engagement, and sincere ethical concerns.

24. I could not have dreamt that there existed a professor—Karen Meyer—in my own department who is as passionate about Jiddu Krishnamurti's work as I am and who has been engaged with his work for over 20 years. Life *is* mysterious! Professor Meyer showed me the importance of patience and love through her pedagogy and for this I am forever thankful.

25. It is crucial to point out here that while Krishnamurti has a definite impact on the way I perceive life and education, his influence on my life is not the reason why I undertook this research, nor has the work anything to do with Krishnamurti and I being from India, nor is there any compensatory or reactionary value attached to the work. Krishnamurti defies, and so do I, the ugly nationalistic divisions, which simply represent the human search for security through wrong means. So in spite of our roots in India, this work has no nationalistic attachments. I have done this work as a student of education to explore the role of the former

in the preservation of humanity and the earth. Moreover, I have not done this work because I have some reactions against those who in a way tried to suppress my interests from "propagandizing" Krishnamurti's thoughts. I truly and honestly intend to share my understanding of Krishnamurti's insights because I think his work has found very little concern with education audiences in spite of his colossal contributions.

2   ON THE NATURE OF CONSCIOUSNESS

1. I am not implying that these political systems are equivalents. However, they draw, in one form or another, their raison d'être in Marxist thinking.

2. By no means am I arguing that Marxist and neo-Marxist analyses of capitalist system and the associated exploitation, inequality, and oppression are invalid. Had it not been for Marx and his followers, we would not be so well informed of how capitalist system functions to create inequalities and injustices in society. However, my perspective differs from Marxist thinking as far as the origin of the capitalist system, the nature of consciousness, and the idea of transformation is concerned.

3. "Structures" here means all the things human beings have created; whereas, "consciousness" means human psyche that is the source of all human thoughts, feelings, and actions. My assertion—"structures are basically crystallized consciousness"—simply means that whatever we, human beings, have produced have to have a source in our consciousness. Thus, if we only focus on understanding the outer world or structures without considering the inner life or consciousness, we are likely to reach flawed conclusions about human conflicts and problems.

4. In this discussion I am confining myself to human consciousness and what it has created in society. Nature—plants, animals, and space—are not included in this particular discussion. Certainly, these beautiful trees outside my window, which are being cut down insanely, exist independent of what I think or do not think about them.

5. It is important to clarify one question, which is often put to me: What about all the good things that human beings have created? It would be important here to consider two major divisions of the discipline of Psychology: cognitive psychology and psychoanalysis. Cognitive psychology emphasizes capacities of mind: its efficiency, memory, creativity, and conceptualization. Psychoanalysis, on the other hand, emphasizes more on the conflicts within different layers of the mind. While these two branches of psychology have

grown rather separately, the human mind has not; it is efficient and conflict-ridden at the same time. It is also fearful, ambitious, and nationalistic. It is capable of producing atomic energy; it is also capable of dropping an atomic bomb. Thus, it would be a blunder to merely appreciate our cognitive capacity and what it creates without making serious efforts to understand and, if possible, eliminate psychological conflicts. Educational institutions at all levels have certainly overstressed the cognitive dimension with almost no attention to the subjective consciousness of individuals (see chapter 3).

6. Undoubtedly, such a perspective has some resonances with psychoanalysis so far as determining the causes of crises are concerned. However, Krishnamurti departs in many of his explanations from psychoanalysis, especially in his ideas of understanding and resolving human conflicts. While for psychoanalysis the conflicts have to be resolved through modifying "Ego," Krishnamurti thinks it is the "Ego" or the "I" which is the root of the trouble.

7. I use the words "consciousness" and "thought" interchangeably following Krishnamurti's expositions regarding this.

8. Such a view of consciousness intrigues many people, like theoretical physicist David Bohm, who would ask Krishnamurti whether there could be a consciousness if thought were absent. Krishnamurti emphasizes that consciousness, as we know it, is made up of all the things it has remembered and it is the result of multiple activities of thought. However, he also remarks that when thought is silent or completely absent, consciousness that exists is entirely different (Krishnamurti and Bohm 1986).

9. See Krishnamurti (1977) and Krishnamurti and Bohm (1999) for an intriguing discussion regarding the process of psychological accumulation.

10. See Bohm (1980) for an intriguing explanation on the relationship of the ancient and modern meanings of "measurement" and human beings' changing perception of reality.

11. The concept of "territorial imperative" (Ardrey 1997) supports such a thesis.

12. By "law" I mean a collective consensus on the common rules of behavior e.g., traffic rules. It would be completely senseless to not see the significance of laws in the smooth functioning of human organizations. Here I am questioning the psychological attitude behind framing laws that define, for example, how a teacher should relate with his/her students. We can have a law that says, "All teachers should have love in their hearts for their pupils." Can love or sensitivity for the other be awakened by means of laws or rules of behavior? A fellow

doctoral student and BEd instructor invited me to her class to present on the idea of "imagination." I was surprised to know that most students believed that human beings cannot have healthy human relationships without the stipulation of laws. (Indeed, they also considered it an absolute necessity that they should be told what to teach and how to teach.) It is my understanding that if I need laws to not exploit or oppress another human being, then I must carefully see if I have soul within me. Is it necessary that only the language of control, regulation, and suppression guide my behavior toward another human being?

13. In his perspective on fear and its wider implications, Krishnamurti seems to adopt an argument similar to psychoanalysis. However, while in psychoanalysis there is no ending to fear except for some reduction in intensity, Krishnamurti (2005b) feels that through deep observation of self and its mechanism without choice, one could completely end or dispel psychological fear, as it arises. He suggests that if one can hold fear and look at it as an "extraordinary jewel" then one begins to see its total structure and movement; and the very seeing of fear is the ending of fear.

14. One may raise this question: But, cannot divergent conditioning influences also cause opportunities for subjective reconstruction? Yes, they can and they do, but subjective reconstruction implies positive modification or incremental change of one's subjectivity over time. From the perspective of meditative inquiry what is key to psychological transformation is not intellectual-critical-reflexive engagement with subjectivity, but an existential observation—without analysis or judgment—of the conditioning processes and their interplay as they influence our thinking, actions, and relationships.

15. Krishnamurti's idea of "conditioning" draws parallel with ideas in Western discourses such as Foucault's "processes of normalization" and "regimes of truth," Bourdieu's "social field" and "habitus," Deleuze's "territorialization," and Lacan's "symbolic order." For Bourdieu there is less likelihood of going beyond conditioning—the deep-seated socialization and habitual processes represented through social field and habitus. Similarly, Lacan considers that the unconscious is structured by language and there is no freedom from conditioning. Foucault and Deleuze, on the other hand, seem more optimistic about the possibilities of modification of our conditioning. According to Foucault, the way out of "processes of normalization" and "regimes of truth" is through critique. Critique, in Foucault's view, is a never-ending process, a practice that questions the precepts/predetermined morals/command-based ethics/a definite

blueprint/existing epistemologies and ontologies/govern-mentality (not the government but mentality to govern/control/regulate). In other words, critique is a rejection of all forms of authority—religious, political, economic, cultural, and institutional. Critique, Foucault thinks, is virtue for it approaches freedom. Deleuze suggests the process of "deterritorialization" to question and possibly go beyond "territorialization." Territorialization implies conforming to the established systems and paradigms that leads to fixity and habituation. Deterritorialization, on the other hand, represents the attempts to question the existing systems and create new assemblages through creative acts, creative thinking, and creative processes. Krishnamurti, however, would argue that "critique" and "deterritorialization" still fall within the field of thought. He would consider these processes to be the agents of "modifications" rather than "radical transformation," which, according to him, is only possible when we perceive our psychological conditioning, fragmentation, and contractions through nonjudgmental, meditative awareness. The process of critique in the psychological sphere will create more contradictions. One part of thought will critique another and the internal conflict will continue. Rather than being critical in the mental sphere, Krishnamurti suggests developing perspicacious awareness of the latter. It is this awareness or perception, rather than any critique or theorization, that breaks the pattern of conditioning inside us, in our actions and relationships, and therefore in the social structures. (For the parallels between Krishnamurti and Western discourses in this endnote I am indebted to late Don MacDougall, a colleague from The University of British Columbia, who actually initiated developing these connections after I conducted a discussion on *The Future of Humanity* (Krishnamurti and Bohm 1986) in fall 2008 in Professor Anne Phelan's Doctoral Seminar in the Department of Curriculum & Pedagogy.)

16. The idea of "the observer is the observed" is one of the most critical perceptions of Krishnamurti in human psychology as acknowledged by psychiatrists like David Shainberg and Benjamin Weinniger in their thinking and medical practice (see Blau 1995). It is also this idea that brought renowned physicist David Bohm close to Krishnamurti and influenced his ideas on wholeness and implicate order, which deny a mechanistic vision of science looking at life and the universe as fragmented instead of a unified whole.

17. Besides, being obsessed with anger or fear and expressing it unconsciously or mechanically is also the movement of becoming as much as it is to repress it. That is, suppression and indulgence are different

forms of becoming. To make the nature of the process of becoming more nuanced, I assert that the constant movement of thought is also a process of becoming. Why is it that thought is never silent? Is not because thought is based on memory, which is past, modifying itself in the present, and projecting into the future without hardly any break? Thus, mind—conscious or unconscious—in actuality is never in the present moment and thus never silent.

18. See Ouspensky (1949) for an authoritative introduction to Gurdjieff's ideas on mind and consciousness.

19. Readers may ask: What would Krishnamurti say to Gandhi or to Jane Addams who devoted their life engaging with violence for decades? In my view, Krishnamurti was no less concerned with nonviolence than Gandhi or Jane Addams or Bertrand Russell. However, Krishnamurti's primary emphasis was to deeply grasp the psychological roots of violence. While it is noble to be concerned with peace and nonviolence, not recognizing that any superficial or structural change cannot transform psyche, where conflicts actually originate, is not more than wishful thinking and premature action.

20. Some scholars would raise questions like these: Cannot fragmentation also lead to generation as well, as implied in the notion of dialectical thinking? Cannot this conflict open up thought to difference and inform a richer or vigorous perception of events? The dialogue within? As in my response to the concern about "subjective reconstruction," I agree that conflict also leads to generation. Creation may have two sources: conflict and silence. In my view, creation that has its roots in conflicts only furthers conflicts, however subtly. It is the creation that grows out of silence and meditation that can bring about peace and integration.

21. See Bohm (1980, 1992) for the intriguing explanation of the fragmentary nature of thought and the society it has created.

22. David Bohm was one of the most influential theoretical physicists and thinkers of our time. His work immensely contributed to the fields of quantum physics, cognition, consciousness studies, communication studies, and science education. He met Krishnamurti in early 1960s and they became close friends until the death of Krishnamurti in 1986. Krishnamurti and Bohm had many dialogues together, which were published in the form of several books. David Bohm also contributed as a member to the Krishnamurti foundations and schools until his death in 1992. See Peat (1997) for a detailed account of the life and works of Bohm.

23. In this work Bohm shares his insights into the nature of mind, consciousness, measure, insight, and meditation to develop his ideas on

fragmentation and wholeness. Bohm duly recognizes Krishnamurti's contributions in explaining the nature of fragmentation and the need for a holistic perspective.

24. One may ask: While accurate, is this observation the final word on "human civilization"? Do not genius, compassion, creativity, heroism, and insight also represent human civilization? Of course, the achievements of science, technology, and arts are breathtaking, but we also need to reconsider whether we have been able to understand and resolve our basic psychological conflicts and problems. Put differently, *has there been a psychological evolution?* Have we been able to deeply understand our fears, conditioning, anger, greed, and violence that dominate our beings and society? *Unless this basic problem—our psychology—is understood and transformed, what is the future of this growing science and technology? We know it: a global suicide, which is approaching us everyday.* Besides, even behind any landmarks in human evolution—such as scientific inventions—it is insight, not thought, from a silent mind that makes "inventions" possible (Krishnamurti and Bohm 1986). So insight, rather than being the product of thinking occurs when one is in a silent, receptive state of mind.

25. Also see Fromm (1969) for more explanations regarding the relationship among fear, identification, and conflict.

26. The famous geographer A. J. Herbertson ([1916] 1996) made an insightful statement almost a century ago questioning the tendency among geographers to consider human beings and nature as inherently separate: "The separation of whole into man [human beings] and in his [their] environment is such a murderous act" (380).

27. In my understanding, a conception of subjectivity that limits it to the experiences, memories, images, thoughts, and emotions, is also materialistic in nature but on a rather subtler level. Anything that one can be aware of is material in a deeper sense. If we can be aware of our thoughts, they are also material forms. They are images of the external things and our projections. That is, they are the "objects" of consciousness. Only awareness (or watchfulness), which is like a mirror, is nonmaterial for it cannot be observed or be aware of. The moment we name it, it ceases to be awareness. Why? Because naming is a process of recognition based on past memory. We cannot recognize something without already having some knowledge about it. Awareness is not related to thought and hence cannot be recognized, except being aware of, existentially speaking. The moment we name it we are back to the realm of thought, which is perfectly alright for the purpose of communication and explanation.

28. There have been several scholars in the West who talk about a reality that exists beyond thought. For example: Heidegger's notions of "beyond" and "silence" and Lacan's notions of "the real" and "the outside" (Pinar, pers. comm.).

3　ON THE NATURE OF EDUCATION

1. There can be no denial about the fact that education has also facilitated enormous technological development and in many cases the ability of resistance to the hegemonic conditioning influences. Nevertheless, it would not be unfair to say that (mis) education, being part of the human consciousness, has also been a major factor behind individual and social deterioration. While pointing out the problems of contemporary education, neither Krishnamurti nor Macdonald expressed any pessimism; on the contrary, they strongly felt that if education is taken seriously, it can function as a great force to create a new human being and a new culture free of barbarism of capitalism, behaviorism, and positivism, or more precisely, the culture of materialism. It was, I am certain, Krishnamurti's trust in the significance of education that he established schools and engaged with students, teachers, and parents throughout his life. It was also Macdonald's conviction regarding the possibilities of transformative education that inspired his research, teaching, and participation in school system.

2. You, the reader, may ask: Does acceptance of authority always have its roots in fear? I think understanding the difference between "psychological authority" and "technical authority" will be useful in this context. There is no harm if one is dependent upon a technical expert, say a musician or a linguist. The problem starts when one becomes psychologically dependent on a figure of authority—say a priest—to know what the right conduct in life is. *Life is so complex that no set of rules or commandments can help one live fully. In fact, all rules, especially psychological ones, fall short of any insight in the face of the intricacies of living.* So it is only the intelligence or awareness—the capacity to perceive and respond to the living situation—that can help us rather than being dependent upon the readymade answers. Why then do I write about Krishnamurti? Krishnamurti is not imposing the rules of living on anybody. He is sharing the insights that he has gathered through experimentation in his life. He, like a scientist, is encouraging us to see for our own selves whether what he is saying holds true in our lives. If his insights hold true, through experimentation—not belief—then the truth is ours, not Krishnamurti's. Authority that fears being questioned and challenged is evil.

3. Interestingly enough, even the common vocabulary of our educational institutions (for Example, exams, tests [standardized and otherwise], grades, doctoral defense, discipline, deadlines, instruction/instructor, grant competitions, and "number" of publications and conference presentations) has much to reveal about the role fear plays in their functioning. I should not be misunderstood here. The forgoing may be and in several cases (including my own) are joyful and maturing experiences, but as I have experienced them through my eyes and those of my students and colleagues, the very structure of our educational institutions is centered on the principle of reward and punishment, which could be further encapsulated in one word: fear.

4. Here Krishnamurti takes a position similar to various types of macro-theories (Whitty 1985)—"correspondence theories" (Bowels and Gintis 1976); "reproduction theories" (Althusser 1971; Bourdieu 1973; Bourdieu and Passeron 1977); and "hegemonic theories" (Gramsci 1971)—that emerged during the mid and late 1970s to explain the relationship between education and the wider social structure. Broadly speaking, these theories consider schools and curriculum political and contested spaces, which not only correspond to and are influenced by hegemonic social, economic, politico-ideological, historical, and cultural forces but also reproduce them. In other words, in a society where economic inequalities are rampant, schools will not only mirror or correspond to the inequalities but also reproduce them further. This view considers schools, teachers, and students as passive agents of reproduction determined by wider political and socioeconomic structures. While Krishnamurti's view regarding conditioning influences are consistent with reproduction theory, his ideas about change never resonated those of reproduction scholars. The major flaw in the thinking of reproduction scholars, whose thinking is primarily rooted in Marxist ideas, is their belief that radical social change is only possible if there is a change in wider socioeconomic structure. In my understanding, radical change in our social structures is only possible via change in our consciousness, which has brought structures into existence (see chapters 2 and 4).

5. One question may arise here: If conditioning influences were so predominant, how can we explain the presence of geniuses throughout human history? In my view, the presence of creative and genius people represents exceptions to the accepted norms. And, more often than not, creative people have had to fight against conditioning influences to carry out their works. That is, creativity or intelligence expresses itself in a rebellious form. It is my contention that if our education can play a significant role in going beyond conditioning influences

in and about ourselves, creative intelligence and expression will not be limited to the "chosen few."

6. I would like to discuss an important aspect of the Indian educational system here in which I studied and taught for 23 years of my life. Perhaps in the developed world there are more opportunities and freedom to follow one's heart, but in India I have seen the creative potentials of children being crushed in front of my own eyes. After grade ten, for example, students and subjects are "streamlined," which I would prefer to call "brutally divided," into science, arts/humanities, and commerce. A great majority of boys and girls who score high on exams, if their parents can afford private tuitions, opt for the "science stream" in order to become engineers and doctors, respectively. The next rung, the "commerce stream," is chosen by those students who score comparatively low grades in the national level examination and who want to pursue careers in business, accounts, and management. The "arts/humanities stream" is mainly selected by those students who score the lowest grades on national level exams. Readers will be surprised to know that many Indian science students at The University of British Columbia as well as in India think that arts/humanities are meant for intellectually inferior students! Grades and parental desires, which in turn are governed by and create social pressures, define children's interest. When children begin school they almost know what they want to become! By means of force we decide what a child should study and thereby cultivate fear instead of creative intelligence. The most tragic fact is that soon children begin to feel that it is not parents and society but they themselves who have chosen the studies they are pursuing. It is the fear of failure, rejection, and punishment that forms the core of our educational institutions, and not only in India.

4   ON THE NATURE OF MEDITATIVE INQUIRY

1. One may ask: What is the problem with the unending nature of analysis? In the study of the material reality (whether crystallized thoughts in the form of human products or nature) constant analysis is the way to accumulate more and more knowledge and extend the frontiers of our minds. However, in the realm of one's psychology or consciousness, analysis is not helpful, because the knowledge that one accumulates out of analysis will become the barrier to further insights. The purpose of analysis is to reach conclusions about the nature of self; self-knowing or meditation, on the other hand, is not accumulative. Its purpose is not to reach conclusions about self. It is simply a constant observation where self, when allowed to be itself

without any suppression or judgment, releases the conflicts it is holding within it. Both self-knowing and analysis are never-ending processes, but the former focuses only on observation of the self without
any judgment whereas the main objective of the latter is to reach
some conclusion and act from that conclusion.

2. One may raise a question: Cannot thought also surpass its past, and be
novel and creative? There are two terms that can help us understand
this question: modification and insight. Certainly, thought has this
extraordinary capacity to modify itself and create new combinations
and permutations. That is how most of our knowledge is extended.
But thought in itself is incapable of "insights," which occur when it
is in a silent or receptive state of mind. Thought, then, takes over the
insights once they have happened and creates new combinations and
permutations (see Bohm 1992). I give more explanations regarding
insights later in the next section of this chapter.

3. "But," one may ask, "do not we need some 'distance' in order to gain
deeper understanding?" Yes, we do, and that is the function of meditation, as I will explain later.

4. See Evelyne Blau's (1995) *Krishnamurti: 100 Years* that elaborately
reports the reminiscences of many world-renowned people from all
walks of life who were drawn toward Krishnamurti's teachings.

5. Heidegger as well as his Canadian admirer, George P. Grant, held
this view that communism is nothing but modified capitalism (Pinar
pers. comm.).

6. See Bohm (1992) for a detailed exploration of similar ideas where he
analyzes the nature of "thought as a system," which governs our life
inwardly and outwardly. According to Nichol (1992):

> The essential relevance of Bohm's redefinition of thought is
> the proposal that body, emotion, intellect, reflex and artifact
> are now understood as *one unbroken field of mutually informing
> thought*. All of these components interpenetrate one another
> to such an extent, says Bohm, that we are compelled to see
> "thought as a system"—concrete as well as abstract, active as
> well as passive, collective as well as individual. (xi; emphasis
> in original)

7. However, it is equally true that when I see the meaning of the word
"religion" as Krishnamurti deals with it, the word loses its ugly relations
with rituals and superstitions, fear and greed, fundamentalism and
dogmatism, heaven and hell, God and priest, and sin and evil. Then
the word signifies to me, as also indicated in (some of) the etymological
explanations, the "gathering of all energy" to "consider carefully" the
nature of reality and one's own self (Krishnamurti 1999a, 33).

8. Negation does not mean brutal destruction of one's thinking mechanism and thoughts. Negation implies understanding that thought is limited, even that of Krishnamurti's and Buddha's; and this very understanding—not just intellectual comprehension, which no doubt is very essential—opens the mind for the new perceptions and intelligence. As Krishnamurti would often say, "My words are like a finger pointing to the moon. Do not limit yourself to the finger, look at the moon!" Likewise, there is a Zen saying addressed to Zen monks: "If you come across Buddha in your meditation, kill him immediately." This "killing" is not destructive in nature, but a negation or an understanding that it is the Ego that is projecting itself as the Buddha or getting attached to the "finger." Negation never implies not studying or contemplating what others, including Krishnamurti or Buddha, have said or authored. If that were the case, none of the teachers would have uttered a single sentence or engaged people in self-inquiry. Study in itself is not problematic as long as one realizes that thought by its very nature is limited and, while it is greatly useful at the level of the material reality, it is problematic when applied blindly to understanding consciousness.

9. It is important to clarify the meaning of change based on self-understanding and why such a change is so important. Some people would argue that change is inevitable even without self-understanding. Some would say even totalitarianism is change. Change in this discussion means a transformation that is not based on a predefined pattern; for, a predefined change considers structures more important than individual subjectivity, as I have already discussed. Moreover, change does not imply a final state to be achieved either at the personal or at the social level. The source of real change is creative understanding of one's own self from moment to moment, which allows it not to be repetitive and mechanical. Change basically means a constant process of self-knowing in relationship to people, things, and nature.

5 ON THE NATURE OF CURRICULUM AS MEDITATIVE INQUIRY

1. Embeddedness (Schachtel 1959) conveys a psychological state of mind when a person, under the threat of new experiences and activities, is aroused emotionally to seek equilibrium, to return to a lack of arousal. Thus, instead of turning outward and exploring the new, he or she turns his or her activity toward restoring the old—either personal or cultural. In either case, the "circuit" is closed to the development of potential and the person is embedded.

2. One may raise these questions here: Is there no situation—for example, rock climbing or gliding—when fear might cultivate attention? Are there no forms of authority—for example, Krishnamurti's moral authority—that encourage openness and responsiveness? While human existence is very complicated, for the sake of understanding the first question, we can say that there are two kinds of fears: biological and psychological. To be in a dangerous situation and having no sense of fear is not fearlessness but lack of intelligence or strong suicidal instinct. Our biological organism has a strong instinct to stay alive and, therefore, jumping out of the way of a car that might kill us, or jumping out of window of a house that is on fire, is simply a self-protective intelligence of the organism. Fear proves crippling when it is primarily psychological in nature. When my whole being trembles only at the utterance of the word "death" without any real danger, fear has taken a form that is highly crippling in nature.

   In response to the second question, it is important to understand the difference between two words: trust and faith. Faith requires of us no intelligence. For example, most religions require us to begin with the assumption that there is a God. This very belief inhibits the inquiry. Authority, when it does not allow itself to be questioned, is very dangerous, because it thrives on borrowed knowledge rather than direct experience. Trust means one neither denies nor accepts but inquires into whatever is being said by anybody including Krishnamurti. It is not belief in what Krishnamurti is saying that brings about "openness" and "personal responsiveness," but my inquiry into what he is saying. If my own experiments show me the truth or falsity of what he is saying, then I may have gratitude for him, but in no way a sense of dependence in his authority. If my trust becomes a faith, then my inquiry has no meaning whatsoever.

3. Macdonald's own personal life and pedagogy reflects these attributes, as is shown in essays published in the 1985 memorial issue (vol. 6, no. 3) of *JCT*.

4. Macdonald's view of "open" school is in contrast with most schools of the contemporary society—primarily functioning as "a degree factory, a credential provider, or a certifier" (Macdonald [1971a] 1995, 41)—that he characterized as "closed." In a closed school, "learning outcomes are synonymous with evaluated performance. Learning is described as conditioning and/or reinforcement, problem solving (with predetermined answers), remembering and recognizing…[Children] are objects to be manipulated and consumers of school goods. The function of the school is simply life adjustment, or occupational preparation, or cultural indoctrination, literacy or

citizenship. Social relationships are primarily bases of confirmation, sanction and motivation; and communication is a process of attending to predetermined stimuli with the production of predictable responses. Everything is, in a sense, inside the reality of prestructured relationship" (Macdonald [1964] 1995, 33).

5. According to Macdonald ([1964] 1995), "purposefulness" can be viewed in many ways including: "higher relatedness" (Buber 1955), "freedom from anxieties" (Tillich 1952) "productivity" (Fromm 1947), and "productive rebellion" (Lindner 1952). "Whatever view of purposefulness we choose, throughout each view," Macdonald notes "runs the thread of freedom and individuality, whether for individual maturities' sake or as the basis for higher relatedness" (Macdonald [1964] 1995,18).

6. While elaborating the importance of developing "self-governance, autonomy, and independence," Macdonald ([1981a] 1995, 161) has also suggested that students and teachers in schools and in academia should be "asked to develop and share their own creative models of educational contexts that are relevant to their own work." This process of developing models involves specifying the "intention of the model" (i.e., control, understanding, or liberation) as well as clarifying the "value assumptions concerning cosmos and human nature." Persons involved are also encouraged to share "what new insights" or "practical implication" their models have for them as well as to engage in mutual criticism for further improvements. Such a curriculum activity—that has freedom, creativity, and sharing at its core—"not only is an exercise of thinking, but of revealing and clarifying values, of searching for new perspectives, and engaging in moral, political, and aesthetic discourses" (161). Freedom to experiment and critically engage with what one feels worthwhile is, undoubtedly, an essential part of a meditative curriculum.

7. Also see Michael Polanyi's *Personal Knowledge: Towards a Post-Critical Philosophy* (1958).

8. In his significant essay—"Curriculum, Consciousness, and Social Change"—Macdonald ([1981a] 1995), drawing upon the Philip Phenix's (1971) concept of "curriculum transcendence" provides further insight into the notion of transcendence. Transcendence implies that teachers and students go beyond "the limitations and restrictions of their social conditioning and common sense and to venture beyond by seeing and choosing new possibilities. Thus the human spirit becomes engaged in the direction of this transcendent activity through the guidance of the meaningfully valued goodness toward which these new possibilities may lead" (Macdonald [1981a] 1995,

159). Encouraging students and teachers to go beyond conditioning has certainly been one of Krishnamurti's major concerns in his lifetime, as I have previously discussed.

9. For Carl Jung's ideas Macdonald referred to De Lazelo (1959).

10. For his understanding of the ways activities are organized in schools, Macdonald draws upon Hall's (1959, 1966, 1976) expositions regarding ten interrelated and dynamic nonverbal systems of culture, which include: interactions, materials, associations, defense, work, play, bisexuality, learning, space, and time.

11. Macdonald borrowed the concept of "meditative thinking" from Martin Heidegger, as described in George Steiner (1978).

12. *Vigyan Bhiarav Tanra* is an ancient Indian text that contains 112 methods of meditation, several of which have visualization and imagination at their core. This ancient Indian text was reproduced in Paul Reps and Nyogen Senzaki's *Zen Flesh, Zen Bones: A Collection of Zen and Pre-Zen Writings* (1957). Osho, in his highly acclaimed *Book of Secrets: 112 Keys to the Mystery Within* (1998), provides detailed explanations of these methods and their significance for contemporary human beings. In my view, *Book of Secrets* is indispensable for anybody interested in understanding the meaning and significance of meditation. *Book of Secrets* is a combined publication of Osho's *Vigyan Bhairav Tantra* published in two volumes. Both these volumes are available online: http://www.messagefrommasters.com/Ebooks/Osho_Books_on_Tantra_&_Mantra.htm.

13. Rabindranath Tagore—a poet, novelist, musician, painter, playwright, and educator, who won a Nobel prize for his collection of poems, *Gitanjali* (1913) (for which preface was written by William Butler Yeats)—built one of the most important alternative educational institutions, Shantiniketan (Abode of Peace), in India centered entirely on the expression of aesthetics and creativity. This school became the nucleus of the Vishva Vidalaya (University), which Tagore founded in 1921 and which, in turn, became a central university after India's independence in 1951 known as Visva Bharti (Communion of the World with India). Tagore's works provide a strong Eastern antecedent to Macdonald's concern for aesthetics that in certain ways was an antecedent to a big sector of curriculum scholarship—understanding curriculum as aesthetic text (Pinar et al., 1995)—in North America.

CONCLUSION

1. While I chose this insightful quote of Macdonald regarding the meaning and significance of theoretical research, it was Professor

Anne Phelan of The University of British Columbia, who revealed to me its importance for my work.

2. While I had studied and also written about Macdonald and his work (A. Kumar, forthcoming), it was Dr. Pinar who actually brought my attention to closely understanding the similarities between Macdonald's and Krishnamurti's works. I was almost astonished as I reread Macdonald to see how closely his ideas resonated with that of Krishnamurti. I actually feel surprised at how Macdonald did not come across the works of people like Krishnamurti, Gurdjieff, and Tagore, who not only share Macdonald's concern but also provide tremendous insights for further exploration. I plan to undertake the task Macdonald left behind in my future research, which is to elaborate his central concerns discussed in the previous chapter.

3. It is important for me to acknowledge that while I am perhaps the first scholar to investigate Krishnamurti's ideas in such detail in curriculum theory, his work has had some presence in curriculum theory (Piirto 1999, 2008; Johnson 2003; Eppert 2008; Kaneda 2008) and a long presence in the philosophy of education in North America. For example: Ching-Chun Han's doctoral dissertation (1991) compares the work of Krishnamurti and Dewey under the supervision of Maxine Greene at Teachers College; and Leelawathie Ayraganie Kobbekaduwa's doctoral dissertation (1990) compares Krishnamurti's educational ideas with Richard Stanley Peters (a renowned philosopher of education from the United Kingdom) under the supervision of F. N. Walker at the University of Alberta. Moreover, Krishnamurti's work has also been incorporated in the field of holistic education (Forbes 1994; Miller 2000; Nakagawa 2000; Rudge 2008). Professor Jack Miller of the Ontario Institute for Studies in Education (University of Toronto), who is a leader in the field of holistic education, has lectured at Krishnamurti's Brockwood Park School in the United Kingdom. Moreover, two of his doctoral students have conducted empirical studies of Krishnamurti's Oak Grove School in Ojai Valley California. At The University of British Columbia, Professor Karen Meyer has employed Krishnamurti's insights in her research (2006, 2010) and in developing a graduate level course called "Living Inquiry," which she has been teaching for almost a decade. In this course, her focus is to encourage students to develop and apply the arts of listening, seeing, and dialogue in their fieldwork. Inspired by Professor Meyer's scholarship, two scholars have undertaken research in this area. One master's student—Misty Ann Paterson (2010)—has submitted her MA thesis based on her research that reports middle school children's favorable responses

NOTES   161

to the pedagogy of living inquiry. Another master's student—Saira
Devji—is in the process of writing her thesis based on her research
work with elementary students wherein she is underscoring the
extraordinary significance of the "pedagogy of listening."

4. While Macdonald's work has been appreciated by curriculum theorists of his time, his work has not been subject to much research in
education. "Of course," Pinar (1985, 43) points out, "Jim and his work
are appreciated... But, I think, not enough. A close re-reading of his
major essays yields a large fact; Jim's work *was* and *is* more important
than many, perhaps most, of us realized." Pinar made his statement
almost 25 years ago, but unfortunately the research production with
reference to Macdonald's work remains very limited. Besides the
present research, the following scholars have explored Macdonald's
work: William Searles's (1982) *JCT* article applies Macdonald's models in the development of science curriculum; Melva M. Burke did
her PhD dissertation—"Reciprocity of Perspectives: An Application
of the Work of James Macdonald to a Personal Perspective of
Special Education" (1983)—in the field of special education at the
University of North Carolina at Greensboro under the supervision
of Dale L. Brubaker; Bernard Spodek (1985) uses Macdonald's
work in the area of early childhood education; and Patricia Holland
and Noreen Garman's (1992) *JCT* essay—"Macdonald and the
Mythopoetic"—extends and problematizes Macdonald's notion of
"mythopoetic imagination" (Macdonald [1981b] 1995, 179). While
there exists limited direct research on Macdonald's work, what is
interesting is that Macdonald's work has subtly, like a "mysterious"
force, affected much of the work in contemporary curriculum studies. His writings that are rooted in the principles of "personal humanism" ([1964] 1995, 1966a, 1966b, 1969) not only were reflected in
the field of curriculum studies during 1970s, but are also present in
subjectivity-oriented scholarships in contemporary curriculum theory, which includes, autobiographical, holistic, humanistic, theological, psychoanalytic, phenomenological, and existentialist approaches;
his concerns for "socio-political humanism" ([1971a] 1995, [1975b]
1995, [1975c] 1995, [1977a] 1995, [1981a] 1995) strongly shares the
concerns of contemporary political theory; his criticisms of radical
and structural theory in education ([1974]1995) found their materialization in the postmodern concerns of the contemporary field;
and the "transcendental" ([1974]1995) concerns of his work can be
found as an important part of theological and holistic discourses in
curriculum theory. Certainly, given the tremendous importance of
Macdonald's work, I think the limited amount of research on him

represents curriculum scholars' obliviousness to the roots of their own scholarship (Pinar 1995; Pinar et al. 1995).

5. Meenakshi Thapan (2006) has conducted a remarkable research of Krishnamurti's Rishi Valley School in India. Kevin M. Cloninger's (2008) doctoral research involved empirical studies at Oak Grove School (Ojai, California) and Brockwood Park School (Brockwood Park, England). In the fall of 2012, I also spent 3 months at Brockwood Park School to complete my research project titled "Understanding the Life-World of a Meditative Education."

A talk and an interview I gave at Brockwood Park School to share my impressions of the nature and character of education there can be accessed from the following links: http://www.youtube.com/watch?v=qKPxp7FtpBU; http://www.brockwood.org.uk/pdf/observer_autumn_winter2012.pdf

References

Allport, Gordon W. 1955. *Becoming: Basic Considerations for a Psychology of Personality*. New Haven: Yale University Press.

Althusser, Louis. 1971. *Lenin and Philosophy and Other Essays*. Translated by Ben Brewster. London: New Left Books.

Aoki, Ted T. 2005. "Teaching as Indwelling between Two Curriculum Worlds." In *Curriculum in a New Key*, edited by William F. Pinar and Rita L. Irwin, 159–165. Mahwah, NJ: Lawrence Erlbaum.

Apple, Michael W. 1985. "There Is a River: James B. Macdonald and Curricular Tradition." *Journal of Curriculum Theorizing* 6 (3): 9–18.

Ardrey, Robert. 1997. *The Territorial Imperative: A Personal Inquiry into the Animal Origins of Property and Nations*. With an introduction by Irvine Devore. 2nd ed. New York: Kodansha America.

Arendt, Hannah. 1958. *The Human Condition*. Chicago: University of Chicago Press.

———. 1977. *Between Past and Future*. New York: Penguin.

Arthus-Bertrand, Yann, dir. 2009. *Home*. Documentary film. Paris: Europa Corp. http://www.youtube.com/watch?v=jqxENMKaeCU.

Balfour-Clarke, Russell. 1977. *The Boyhood of J. Krishnamurti*. Bombay: Chetana.

Blackburn, Gabriele. 1996. *The Light of Krishnamurti*. Ojai, CA: Idylwild Books.

Blau, Evelyne. 1995. *Krishnamurti: 100 Years*. New York: A Joost Elffers Book.

Bobbitt, Franklin. 1918. *The Curriculum*. New York: Houghton Mifflin.

Bohm, David. 1980. *Wholeness and the Implicate Order*. London: Routledge.

———. 1992. *Thought as a System*. Foreword by Lee Nichol. London: Routledge.

———. 1996. *On Dialogue*. Foreword by Lee Nichol. London: Routledge.

———. 1998. *On Creativity*. Foreword by Lee Nichol. London: Routledge.

———. 1999. "Preface: An Introduction to Krishnamurti's Work." In *The Limits of Thought: Discussions between J. Krishnamurti and David Bohm*, edited by R. McCoy, vii–x. London: Routledge.

Bourdieu, Pierre. 1973. "Cultural Reproduction and Social Reproduction." In *Knowledge, Education and Cultural Change: Papers in the Sociology of Education*, edited by Richard K. Brown, 71–112. London: Tavistock Publications.

Bourdieu, Pierre, and Jean-Claude Passeron. 1977. *Reproduction in Education, Society and Culture*. Translated by Richard Nice. Beverly Hills, CA: Sage.

Boutte, Veronica. 2002. *The Phenomenology of Compassion in the Teachings of Jiddu Krishnamurti*. Lewiston: Edwin Mellen.

Bowels, Samuel, and Herbert Gintis. 1976. *Schooling in Capitalist America: Educational Reform and the Contradictions of Economic Life*. New York: Basic Books.

Brook, Peter, dir. 1979. *Meetings with Remarkable Men: Guardieff's Search for Hidden Knowledge*. Film. New York: Parabola Video. http://video .google.com/videoplay?docid=-3813872527827778135#.

Brubaker, Dale L., and Gayle Brookbank. 1986. "James Macdonald: A Bibliography." *Journal of Curriculum & Supervision* 1 (3): 215–220.

Brueggemann, Walter. 2001. *The Prophetic Imagination*. 2nd ed. Minneapolis, MN: Fortress Press.

Buber, Martin. 1955. *Between Man and Man*. Boston: Beacon Press.

Burke, Melva M. 1983. "Reciprocity of Perspectives: An Application of the Work of James B. Macdonald to a Personal Perspective of Special Education." PhD diss., University of North Carolina, Greensboro.

———. 1985. "The Personal and Professional Journey of James B. Macdonald." *Journal of Curriculum Theorizing* 4 (1): 84–119.

Chandmal, Asit. 1985. *One Thousand Moons: Krishnamurti at Eighty-Five*. New York: Harry N Abrams. Also published in 1995, with additional material and updates, as *One Thousand Suns: Krishnamurti at Eighty-Five and the Last Walk*. New York: Aperture.

Christian, William. 1996. *George Grant: A Biography*. Toronto: University of Toronto Press.

Cloninger, Kevin M. 2008. "Transcending Curriculum Ideologies: Educating Human Beings Well." PhD diss., University of Denver, Colorado.

Cohen, Avraham, Marion Porath, Anthony Clarke, Heesoon Bai, Carl Leggo, and Karen Meyer. 2012. *Speaking of Teaching...Inclinations, Inspirations and Innerworkings*. Rotterdam: Sense Publications.

De Lazelo, Violet S., ed. 1959. *The Basic Writings of C. G. Jung*. New York: Modern Library.

Delkhah, M. 1997. "The Pure Man, Discipline of Non: Positioning Grotowski's Metaphysics in Contemporary Euro-Asian Mysticism as Represented by Krishnamurti." PhD diss., University of Kansas, Lawrence.

Dewey, John. 1930. *Individualism: Old and New*. New York: G. P. Putnam's Sons.

Dhopeshwarkar, Atmaram Dhondo. (1967) 1993. *J. Krishnamurti and Awareness in Action*. Bombay: Popular Prakashan.

Eppert, Claudia. 2008. "Fear, (Educational) Fictions of Character, and Buddhist Insights for an Arts-Based Witnessing Curriculum." In *Cross-Cultural Studies in Curriculum: Eastern Thoughts, Educational Insights*, edited by Claudia Eppert and Hongyu Wang, 55–108. New York: Lawrence Erlbaum.

Field, Sidney, and Peter Hay. 1989. *Krishnamurti: The Reluctant Messiah*. New York: Paragon House.

Forbes, Scott H. 1994. "Education as a Religious Activity: Krishnamurti's Insights into Education." www.holistic-education.net/articles/kinsight.pdf.

Freire, Paulo. 1973. *Pedagogy of the Oppressed*. New York: Seabury Press.

———. 1996a. *Education for Critical Consciousness*. New York: Continuum.

———. 1996b. *Pedagogy of Hope*. New York: Continuum.

———. 1998. *Pedagogy of Freedom: Kinds of Knowledge Essential for Educative Practice*. Lanham, MD: Rowman and Littlefield.

Fromm, Erich. 1947. *Man for Himself*. New York: Holt, Reinhold and Winston.

———. 1968. *The Revolution of Hope*. New York: Harper and Row.

———. 1969. *Escape from Freedom*. New York: Henry Holt.

Gadamer, Hans-Georg. 1976. *Philosophical Hermeneutics*. Berkeley: University of California Press.

Giroux, Henry A. 1981. *Ideology, Culture and the Process of Schooling*. Basingstoke, Hampshire: Falmer Press.

———. 1983. *Theory and Resistance in Education*. London: Heinemann Educational Books.

———. 1989. *Schooling, Citizenship and Struggle for Democracy*. London: Routledge.

Goffman, Erving. 1961. *Asylums: Essays on Social Situation of Mental Patients and Other Inmates*. New York: Anchor Books, Doubleday.

Govindon, Aravindan, dir. 1985. *The Seer Who Walks Alone*. Documentary film. Mumbai: Films Division. http://www.youtube.com/watch?v=XKb9pvVarHE.

Gramsci, Atonio. 1971. *Selections from Prison Notebooks*. New York: International Publishers.

Grant, George. 1998 (1974). *English-Speaking Justice*. Toronto: Anansi.

Grego, Richard Forrest. 1997. "Jiddu Krishnamurti and Thich Nhat Hanh on the Silence of God and the Human Condition." PhD diss., State University of New York, Albany.

Grohe, Friedrich. 2001. *The Beauty of the Mountain: Memories of Krishnamurti*. Brockwood Park, Hampshire: Krishnamurti Foundation Trust.

Grumet, Madeleine R. 1976a. "Existential and Phenomenological Foundations." In *Toward a Poor Curriculum*, edited by William F. Pinar and Madeleine R. Grumet, 31–50. Dubuque, IA: Kendall/Hunt.

———. 1976b. "Psychoanalytic Foundations." In *Toward a Poor Curriculum*, edited by William F. Pinar and Madeleine Grumet, 111–146. Dubuque, IA: Kendall/Hunt.

———. 1985. "The Work of James B. Macdonald: Theory Fierce with Reality." *Journal of Curriculum Theorizing* 6 (3): 19–27.

Gurdjieff, George I. 1950. *Beelzebub's Tales to His Grandson: An Objectively Impartial Criticism of the Life of Man*. New York: Harcourt.

———. 1963. *Meetings with Remarkable Men*. London: Routledge.

———. 1975. *Life Is Real Only, Then, When "I Am"* New York: Triangle Editions.

Hall, Edward T. 1959. *The Silent Language*. Garden City, NY: Doubleday.

———. 1966. *The Hidden Dimension*. Garden City, NY: Doubleday.

———. 1976. *Beyond Culture*. Garden City, NY: Doubleday.

Han, Ching-Chun. 1991. "Comparing the 'Educated Person' Conceptions of Dewey and Krishnamurti: Implications for the Republic of China." PhD diss., Columbia University, New York.

Heber, Lilly. 1935. *Krishnamurti and the World Crisis*. London: G. Allen & Unwin.

Heidegger, Martin. 1966. *Discourses on Thinking*. New York: Harper and Row.

Herbertson, A. J. (1915) 1996. "Region, Place and Locality: Regional Environment, Heredity, and Consciousness." In *Human Geography: An Essential Anthology*, edited by John A. Agnew, David N. Livingstone, and Alisdair Rogers, 378–384. Oxford: Blackwell. Originally published in *Geographical Teacher*, 1915, 8: 147–53.

Holden, Lawrence Kirk. 1972. "The Structure of Krishnamurti's Phenomenological Observations and Its Psychological Implications." PhD diss., United States International University, Nairobi, Kenya.

Holland, Patricia, and Noreen B. Garman. 1992. "Macdonald and the Mythopoetic." *Journal of Curriculum Theorizing* 9(4): 45–72.

Holroyd, Stuart. 1980. *The Quest of the Quiet Mind: The Philosophy of Krishnamurti*. Wellinborough: Aquarian Press.

———. 1991. *Krishnamurti: The Man, the Mystery & the Message*. Shaftsbury, Dorset: Element.

Huebner, Dwayne E. 1976. "The Moribund Curriculum Field: Its Wake and Our Work." *Curriculum Inquiry*, 6(2), 153–167.

———. 1985. "The Redemption of Schooling: The Work of James B. Macdonald." *Journal of Curriculum Theorizing* 6 (3): 28–34.

James, William. 1917. *The Will to Believe and Other Popular Essays in Philosophy*. New York and London: Longmans, Green.

Jayakar, Pupul. 1986. *Krishnamurti: A Biography*. San Francisco: Harper & Row.

Johnson, Andrew P. 2003. *Language Arts and the Inner Curriculum*. Detroit: Whole Schooling Consortium.

Kalsi, Ashutosh. 2007. "The Ending of Nihilism: From Nietzsche to Krishnamurti." PhD diss., State University of New York at Buffalo.

Kaneda, Takuya. 2008. "Shanti, Peacefulness of Mind." In *Cross-Cultural Studies in Curriculum: Eastern Thoughts, Educational Insights*, edited by Claudia Eppert and Hongyu Wang, 171–192. New York: Lawrence Erlbaum.

Khattar, Randa. 2001. "Creativity as the Impulse of Life: Scholarly Philosophies and Thoughts for Education." Master's thesis, York University, Toronto.

Kincheloe, Joe L. 2003. *Critical Pedagogy*. New York: Peter Lang.

Kobbekaduwa, Leelawathie Ayraganie. 1990. "Education and the Educated Person: A Comparison of J. Krishnamurti and R. S. Peters." PhD diss., University of Alberta, Edmonton.

Krishnamurti, Jiddu. 1910. *At the Feet of the Master: Towards Discipleship*. Madras: Theosophical Publishing House.

———. 1912. *Education as Service*. Chicago: Rajput Press.

———. 1929. *The Dissolution of the Order of the Star: A Statement*. Ommen, The Netherlands: Star Pub. Trust. http://www.jkrishnamurti .org/about-krishnamurti/dissolution-speech.php.

———. 1953. *Education and the Significance of Life*. London: Victor Gollancz.

———. 1954. *The First and Last Freedom*. Foreword by Aldous Huxley. New York: Harper and Brothers.

———. 1963. *Life Ahead: On Learning and the Search for Meaning*. New York: Harper & Row.

———. 1964. *This Matter of Culture*. Edited by D. Rajagopal. New York: Harper & Row. Also published under the title *Think on These Things*. Ojai, California: Krishnamurti Foundation of America.

———. 1968. *Talks with American Students*. Wassenaar, The Netherlands: Servire.

———. 1969. *Freedom from the Known*. Edited by Mary Lutyens. New York: Harper & Row.

Krishnamurti, Jiddu. 1970. *The Urgency of Change*. Edited by Mary Lutyens. New York: Harper & Row.

Krishnamurti, Jiddu. 1972. *You Are the World: An Authentic Report of Talks and Discussions in American Universities*. New York: Harper & Row.

———. 1973. *The Awakening of Intelligence*. San Francisco: HarperCollins.

———. 1974. *Krishnamurti on Education*. New Delhi: Orient Longman.

———. 1975. *Beginnings of Learning*. London: Gollancz.

———. 1976. *Inward Flowering*. Madras: Krishnamurti Foundation of India.

———. 1977. *Truth & Actuality*. Madras: Krishnamurti Foundation of India.

———. (1979) 2005. *Transformation of Man*. San Francisco: Harper & Row.

———. 1982. "Krishnamurti on Education." In *Within the Mind: On J. Krishnamurti*, edited by Pupul Jayakar and Sunanda Patwardhan. Chennai: Krishnamurti Foundation of India.

———. 1983. *The Network of Thought*. Wassenaar: Mirananda.

———. 1984. "World Peace." Address to the United Nations, New York, April. http://www.krishnamurtiaustralia.org/articles/world_peace.htm. For a video recording see: http://www.guba.com/watch/3000138398.

———. 1991a. *The Art of Listening*. Collected Works Vol. 1 (1933–1934). Dubuque, IA: Kendall-Hunt.

———. 1991b. *Choiceless Awareness*. Collected Works Vol. 5 (1948–1949). Dubuque, IA: Kendall-Hunt.

———. 1991c. *Crisis in Consciousness*. Collected Works Vol. 11 (1958–1960). Dubuque, IA: Kendall-Hunt.

———. 1992. *Mirror of Relationship: Love, Sex and Chastity*. Edited by Douglas Evans and Frode Steen. Ojai, CA: Krishnamurti Foundation of America.

———. 1993. *A Flame of Learning*. Hampshire: Krishnamurti Foundation Trust.

———. 1999a. *This Light in Oneself: True Meditation*. Boston: Shambhala.

———. 1999b. *A Timeless Spring: Krishnamurti at Rajghat*. Edited by Ahalya Chari and Radhika Herzberger. Chennai: Krishnamurti Foundation India.

———. 2001. *What are You Doing with Your Life?* Edited by Dale Carson and Kishore Khairnar. Ojai, CA: Krishnamurti Foundation of America.

———. 2002. *Meditations*. Boston: Shambhala.

———. 2004. *Krishnamurti for the Young: A Series of Three Books*. Edited by Ahalya Chari. Chennai: Krishnamurti Foundation of India.

———. 2005a. *Facing a World in Crisis*. Boston: Shambala.

———. 2005b. *Seeing Fear as an Extraordinary Jewel*. Video recording of address. Bramdean, Hampshire: Krishnamurti Foundation Trust.

———. 2006. *Whole Movement of Life Is Learning: J. Krishnamurti's Letters to His Schools*. Edited by Ray McCoy. Bramdean, Hampshire: Krishnamurti Foundation Trust.

Krishnamurti, Jiddu, and Allan W. Anderson. 2000. *A Wholly Different Way of Living*. Chennai: Krishnamurti Foundation of India.

Krishnamurti, Jiddu, and Chögyam Trungpa Rinpoche. 1996. "What Is Meditation?" In *Questioning Krishnamurti: J. Krishnamurti in Dialogue with Leading Twentieth Century Thinkers*, edited by David Skitt, 236–242. Bramdean Hampshire: Krishnamurti Foundation Trust.

Krishnamurti, Jiddu, and David Bohm. 1985. *The Ending of Time*. San Francisco: Harper & Row.

———. 1986. *The Future of Humanity: A Conversation*. New York: HarperCollins.

———. 1999. *The Limits of Thought*. Edited by Ray McCoy. London: Routledge.

Krishnamurti, Jiddu, and Huston Smith. 1996. "Can One have Lucidity in This Confused World?" In *Questioning Krishnamurti: J. Krishnamurti in Dialogue with Leading Twentieth Century Thinkers*, edited by David Skitt, 200–214. Bramdean, Hampshire: Krishnamurti Foundation Trust.

Krohnen, Michael. 1996. *The Kitchen Chronicles: 1001 Lunches with Krishnamurti*. Ojai, CA: Edwin House.

Kumar, Ashwani. 2007. "Reflexivity and Critical Thinking in Secondary School Social Science: A Study of Transition between Two Alternative Perspectives in Curricular Practice." Master's thesis, University of Delhi, New Delhi, India.

———. 2008a. "Place of Critical Self-Awareness in Social Education for Revolution." Rouge Forum Conference proceedings. http://richgibson.com/rouge_forum/2008/placecritical.htm.

———. 2008b. Review Essay of *Neoliberalism and Education Reform*, edited by E. Wayne Ross and Rich Gibson. *Journal of Critical Education Policy Studies* 6 (2): 218–236. http://www.jceps.com/index.php?pageID=article&articleID=139.

———. 2008c. Review of *Social Education in Asia: Critical Issues and Multiple Perspectives*, edited by David L. Grossman and Joe Tin-Yau Lo. *Education Review: A Journal of Book Reviews*. http://edrev.asu.edu/reviews/rev715.htm.

———. 2009. "Social Studies in the Postmodern World: An Essay Review." *Education Review: A Journal of Book Reviews* 12 (10). http://edrev.asu.edu/essays/v12n10index.html.

———. 2010. "A Synoptic View of Curriculum Studies in South Africa. *Journal of the American Association for the Advancement of Curriculum Studies* 6. Retrieved on March 13, 2011. http://www2.uwstout.edu/content/jaaacs/Kumar_V6.htm.

Kumar, Ashwani. 2011a. "Curriculum Studies in Brazil: An Overview." In *Curriculum Studies in Brazil*, edited by William F. Pinar, 27–42. New York: Palgrave Macmillan.

———. 2011b. "Curriculum Studies in Mexico: An Overview." In *Curriculum studies in Mexico*, edited by William F. Pinar, 29–48. New York: Palgrave Macmillan.

———. 2012. "Indian Social Studies Curriculum in Transition: Effects of a Paradigm Shift in Curriculum Discourse. *Transnational Curriculum Inquiry* 9(1): 20–53. http://ojs.library.ubc.ca/index.php/tci/article/view/2363

———. 2013. "Education as a Political Tool in Asia: An Essay Review." *Asia Pacific Journal of Education*. doi:10.1080/02188791.2012.757418.

———. Forthcoming. "Essentials of a Transformative Curriculum: The Life and Work of James B. Macdonald."

Kumar, Krishna. 2001. *Prejudice and Pride*. New Delhi: Penguin.

———. 2007. *Battle for Peace*. New Delhi: Penguin.

Lall, Marie, and Edward Vickers, eds. 2009. *Education as a Political Tool in Asia*. London: Routledge.

Levinson, Natasha. 2001. "The Paradox of Natality: Teaching in the Midst of Belatedness." In *Hannah Arendt and Education*, edited by Gordon Mordechai, 11–36. Boulder, CO: Westview.

Lindner, Robert. 1952. *Prescription for Rebellion*. New York: Rinehart.

Lutyens, Emily. 1957. *Candles in the Sun*. London: R. Hart-Davis.

Lutyens, Mary. 1975. *Krishnamurti: The Years of Awakening*. London: John Murray.

———. 1983. *Krishnamurti: The Years of Fulfillment*. London: John Murray.

———. 1988. *The Open Door*. London: John Murray.

———. 1990. *The Life and Death of Krishnamurti*. London: John Murray.

———. 1996. *Krishnamurti and the Rajagopals*. Ojai, CA: Krishnamurti Foundation of America.

Macdonald, James B. 1956. "Some Contributions of a General Behavior Theory for Curriculum." PhD diss., University of Wisconsin, Madison.

———. 1958. "Practice Grows from Theory and Research." *Childhood Education* 34 (6): 256–258.

———. (1964) 1995. "An Image of Man." In *Theory as a Prayerful Act: The Collected Essays of James B. Macdonald*, edited by Bradley J. Macdonald, 15–36. New York: Peter Lang. Originally published in *Individualizing Instruction*, edited by Ronald C. Doll, 29–49. (Washington, DC: Association for Supervision and Curriculum Development.)

———. 1966a. "Language, Meaning, and Motivation: An Introduction." In *Language and Meaning: Papers*, edited by James B. Macdonald and Robert Rosborough Leeper, 1–7. Washington, DC: Association for Supervision and Curriculum Development.

———. 1966b. "Person in the Curriculum." In *Precedents and Promise in the Curriculum Field,* edited by Helen F. Robinson, 38–52. New York: Teachers College Press.

———. 1969. "A Proper Curriculum for the Young Children." *Phi Delta Kappan,* 50, March, 406–408.

———. (1971a) 1995. "The School as a Double Agent." In *Theory as a Prayerful Act: The Collected Essays of James B. Macdonald,* edited by Bradley J. Macdonald, 37–48. New York: Peter Lang. Originally published in *Freedom, Bureaucracy and Schooling,* edited by Vernon F. Haubrich, 245–256 (Washington, DC: Association for Supervision and Curriculum Development).

———. (1971b) 1995. "A Vision of the Humane School: An Image of Man." In *Theory as a Prayerful Act: The Collected Essays of James B. Macdonald,* edited by Bradley J. Macdonald, 49–68. New York: Peter Lang. Originally published in *Removing Barriers to Humanness in High School,* edited by J. Galon Saylor and Joshua L. Smith, 2–20 (Washington, DC: Association for Supervision and Curriculum Development).

———. (1974) 1995. "A Transcendental Development Ideology of Education." In *Theory as a Prayerful Act: The Collected Essays of James B. Macdonald,* edited by Bradley J. Macdonald, 69–98. New York: Peter Lang. Originally published in *Heightened Consciousness, Cultural Revolution and Curriculum Theory,* edited by William. F. Pinar, 85–116 (Berkeley, CA: McCutchan).

———. 1975a. "Autobiographical Statement." In *Curriculum Theorizing: The Reconceptualists,* edited by William F. Pinar, 3–4. Berkley, CA: McCutchan.

———. (1975b) 1995. "Curriculum and Human Interest." In *Theory as a Prayerful Act: The Collected Essays of James B. Macdonald,* edited by Bradley J. Macdonald, 99–110. New York: Peter Lang. Originally published in *Curriculum Theorizing: The Reconceptualists,* edited by William F. Pinar, 282–294 (Berkeley, CA: McCutchan).

———. (1975c) 1995. "Quality of Everyday Life in Schools." In *Theory as a Prayerful Act: The Collected Essays of James B. Macdonald,* edited by Bradley J. Macdonald, 111–126. New York: Peter Lang. Originally published in *Schools in Search of Meaning,* edited by James B. Macdonald and Esther Zaret, 78–94 (Washington, DC: Association for Supervision and Curriculum Development).

———. (1977a) 1995. "Living Democratically in Schools: Cultural Pluralism." In *Theory as a Prayerful Act: The Collected Essays of James B. Macdonald,* edited by Bradley J. Macdonald, 127–136. New York: Peter Lang. Originally published in *Multicultural Education: Commitments, Issues, and Applications,* edited by Carl A. Grant, 6–13 (Washington, DC: Association for Supervision and Curriculum Development).

Macdonald, James B. (1977b) 1995. "Value Basis and Issues for Curriculum." In *Theory as a Prayerful Act: The Collected Essays of James B. Macdonald*, edited by Bradley J. Macdonald, 137–148. New York: Peter Lang. Originally published in *Curriculum Theory*, edited by Alex Molnar and John A. Zahorik, 10–21 (Washington, DC: Association for Supervision and Curriculum Development).

———. (1981a) 1995. "Curriculum, Consciousness and Social Change." *Theory as a Prayerful Act: The Collected Essays of James B. Macdonald*, edited by Bradley J. Macdonald, 153–176. New York: Peter Lang. Originally published in *Journal of Curriculum Theorizing* 3 (1): 143–153.

———. (1981b) 1995. "Theory, Practice and the Hermeneutic Circle." In *Theory as a Prayerful Act: The Collected Essays of James B. Macdonald*, edited by Bradley J. Macdonald, 173–186. New York: Peter Lang. Originally published in *Journal of Curriculum Theorizing* 3 (2): 130–138.

———. 1986. "The Domain of Curriculum." Foreword by Dorothy Huencke. *Journal of Curriculum & Supervision* 1 (3): 205–214.

———. 1995. *Theory as a Prayerful Act: The Collected Essays of James B. Macdonald*. Edited by Bradley J. Macdonald. With an introduction by William F. Pinar. New York: Peter Lang.

MacMurray, John. 1958. *Freedom in the Modern World*. London: Faber & Faber.

Mansbridge, Jane, and Aldon Morris, eds. 2001. *Oppositional Consciousness: The Subjective Roots of Social Protest*. Chicago: University of Chicago Press.

Martin, Donald Wesley. 1975. "An Analysis of Selected Works of Jiddu Krishnamurti: Implications for Higher Education." PhD diss., University of Connecticut, Storrs.

Martin, Raymond. 1997. Introduction to *Krishnamurti: Reflections on the Self*, edited by Raymond Martin, xi–xix. Chicago: Open Court.

———. 2003. *On Krishnamurti*. Belmont, CA: Wadsworth.

McLaren, Peter. (1994) 2006. *Life in Schools: An Introduction to Critical Pedagogy in the Foundations of Education*. 3rd ed. New York: Longman.

McLaren, Peter, and Joe L. Kincheloe. 2007. *Critical Pedagogy: Where Are We Now?* New York: Peter Lang.

Mendizza, Michael, dir. 1984. *Krishnamurti: The Challenge of Change*. Documentary film. Narrated by Richard Basehart. Ojai, California: Krishnamurti Foundation of America. http://www.jkrishnamurti.org /krishnamurti-teachings/view-video/the-challenge-of-change-full-version .php.

———, dir. 1990. *Krishnamurti: With a Silent Mind*. Documentary Film. Ojai, California: Krishnamurti Foundation of America. http://www .youtube.com/watch?v=YGJNqp7px3U&feature=relmfu.

Meyer, Karen. 2006. "Living Inquiry—A Gateless Gate and a Beach." In *Spirituality, Ethnography, and Teaching: Stories from Within*, edited by Will Ashton and Diana Denton, 156–166. New York: Peter Lang.

———. 2010. "Living Inquiry: Me, Myself and Other." *Journal of Curriculum Theorizing* 26 (1): 85–96.

Meyer, Karen, and Lynn Margaret Fels. 2009. "Breaking Out: Learning Research from the Women in Prison Project." *International Review of Qualitative Research* 2 (2): 269–290.

Miller, Henry. 1969. "Krishnamurti." In *Books in My Life*, 147–159. New York: New Directions.

Miller, John P. 2000. "Krishnamurti and Holistic Education." *Encounter* 13 (4): 36–45.

Moffatt, Ron. 1976. "Psychotherapy and Krishnamurti: Beyond West and East." Master's thesis, University of Delaware, Newark.

Molnar, Alex. 1985. "Tomorrow the Shadow on the Wall Will Be That of Another." *Journal of Curriculum Theorizing* 6 (3): 35–42.

Nakagawa, Yoshiharu. 2000. "Eastern Philosophy and Holistic Education." PhD diss., Ontario Institute for Studies in Education, University of Toronto.

Narayan, Giddu. 1999. *As the River Joins the Ocean: Reflections about J. Krishnamurti*. Ojai, CA: Edwin House.

Nearing, Helen. 1992. *Loving and Leaving the Good Life*. White River Jct., VT: Chelsea Green.

Needleman, Jacob. 1970. "A Note on Krishnamurti." In *The New Religions*, edited by Jacob Needleman, 145–162. New York: Doubleday.

Nichol, Lee. 1992. Foreword to *Thought as a System* by David Bohm, ix–xv. London: Routledge.

Osho. 1989. *Dhyan Sutra (Principles of Meditation)*. Pune: Tao Publishing.

———. 1996. *Meditation: The First and the Last Freedom*. New York: St. Martin's.

———. 1998. *Book of Secrets: 112 Keys to the Mystery Within*. New York: St.Martin Griffin.

Ouspensky, Peter D. 1949. *In Search of the Miraculous: Fragments of an Unknown Teaching*. New York: Harcourt, Brace.

Paterson, Misty Anne. 2010. "Living Inquiry as Pedagogy." Master's thesis, University of British Columbia, Vancouver.

Patwardhan, Sunanda. 1999. *A Vision of the Sacred: My Personal Journey with Krishnamurti*. Ojai, CA: Edwin House.

Peat, David F. 1997. *Infinite Potential: The Life and Times of David Bohm*. Reading, MA: Addison Wesley.

Phenix, Philip Henry. 1971. "Transcendence and the Curriculum." *Teachers College Record* 73 (2): 271–284.

Piirto, Jane. 1999. "Implications of Postmodern Curriculum Theory for the Education of the Talented." *Journal of the Education of the Gifted* 22 (4): 324–353.

———. 2008. "Krishnamurti and Me: Meditations on His Philosophy of Curriculum and on India." In *Cross-Cultural Studies in Curriculum: Eastern Thoughts, Educational Insights,* edited by Claudia Eppert and Hongyu Wang, 247–266. New York: Lawrence Erlbaum.

Pinar, William F. 1974a. "*Currere:* Toward Reconceptualization." In *Basic Problems in Modern Education: The Second Yearbook of the Arizona Association for Supervision and Curriculum Development,* edited by James John Jelinek, 147–171. Tempe, AZ: Arizona Association for Supervision and Curriculum Development.

———. 1974b. *Heightened Consciousness, Cultural Revolution and Curriculum Theory: The Proceedings of the Rochester Conference.* Berkeley, CA: McCutchan.

———. 1985. "A Prayerful Act: The Work of James B. Macdonald." *Journal of Curriculum Theorizing* 6 (3): 43–53.

———. 1995. Introduction to *Theory as a Prayerful Act: The Collected Essays of James B. Macdonald,* edited by Bradley J. Macdonald, 1–13. New York: Peter Lang.

———. 2004. *What Is Curriculum Theory?* London: Lawrence Erlbaum.

———. 2009a. "Primacy of the Particular." In *Leaders in Curriculum Studies,* edited by Edmund C. Short and Leanard J. Waks, 143–152. Rotterdam: Sense Publishers.

———. 2009b. "Unadressed 'I' of the Ideology Critique." *Power and Knowledge* 1 (2): 189–200.

———. 2009c. *The Worldliness of a Cosmopolitan Education.* London: Routledge.

———. 2012. *What Is Curriculum Theory?* 2nd ed. New York: Routledge.

Pinar, William F., and Madelaine R. Grumet. 1976. *Toward a Poor Curriculum.* Dubuque, IA: Kendall/Hunt.

Pinar, William F., William M. Reynolds, Patrick Slattery, and Peter M. Taubman. 1995. *Understanding Curriculum: An Introduction to Historical and Contemporary Curriculum Discourses.* New York: Peter Lang.

Polanyi, Michael. 1958. *Personal Knowledge: Towards a Post-Critical Philosophy.* Chicago: University of Chicago Press.

———. 1967. *The Tacit Dimension of Knowledge.* Garden City, NY: Doubleday Anchor Books.

Read, Herbert. 1956. *Education through Art.* London: Faber & Faber.

Reps, Paul, and Nyogen Senzaki, comp. 1957. *Zen Flesh, Zen Bones: A Collection of Zen and Pre-Zen Writings.* Boston: Tuttle.

Richards, Mary Caroline. 1962. *Centering: In Pottery, Poetry, and the Person.* Middletown, CN: Wesleyan University Press.

Ricoeur, Paul. 2004. *Memory, History, Forgetting.* Chicago: University of Chicago Press.

Robinson, Ken. 2001. *Out of Our Minds: Learning to be Creative.* Oxford: Capstone.

———. 2009. *The Element: How Finding Your Passion Changes Everything.* New York: Viking.

Rodrigues, Hillary. 1990. *Insights into Religious Mind: An Analysis of Krishnamurti's Thoughts.* New York: Peter Lang.

Rogers, Carl C. 1961. *On Becoming a Person.* Boston: Houghton-Miffin.

———. 1962. "The Interpersonal Relationship: Core of Guidance. *Harvard Educational Review* 32 (4): 416–429.

Rommelaere, Jacques E. H. M. 1976. "A Comparative Study of the Educational Theories of Mohandas Gandhi and Jiddu Krishnamurti." PhD diss., University of Connecticut, Storrs.

Ross, Joseph E. 2000. *Krishnamurti: The Taormina Seclusion 1912.* Bloomington, IN: XLibris.

Ross, E. Wayne, and Rich Gibson, eds. 2007. *Neoliberalism and Education Reform.* Cresskill, NJ: Hampton Press.

Roszak, Theodore. 1970. "Educating Contra Naturam." In *A Man for Tomorrow's World,* edited by Robert R. Leeper, 12–27. Washington, DC: Association for Supervision and Curriculum Development.

Rousseau, Jean-Jacques. 1954. *The Social Contract.* Edited by Charles Frankell. New York: Hafner.

Rudge, Lucila T. 2008. "Holistic Education: An Analysis of Its Pedagogical Application." PhD diss., The Ohio State University, Columbus.

Sabzevary, Amir. 2008. "Choiceless Awareness through Psychological Freedom in the Philosophy of Krishnamurti." PhD diss., California Institute of Intergral Studies, San Francisco.

Sanat, Aryel. 1999. *The Inner Life of Krishnamurti: Private Passion and Perennial Wisdom.* Wheaton, IL: Quest Books.

Schachtel, Ernest. 1959. *Metamorphosis.* New York: Basic Books.

Schwab, Joseph J. 1970. *The Practical: A Language for Curriculum.* Washington DC: Centre for the Study of Education, National Education Association.

Searles, W. E. 1982. "A Substantiation of Macdonald's Models in Science Curriculum Development." *Journal of Curriculum Theorizing* 4 (1): 127–155.

Sloss, Radha Rajagopal. 1991. *Lives in the Shadow with J. Krishnamurti.* London: Bloomsbury.

Smith, Ingram. 1989. *Truth Is a Pathless Land: A Journey with Krishnamurti.* Adyar, Chennai: Theosophical Publishing House. Also published in 1999, with additional material and updates, as *The Transparent Mind: A Journey with Krishnamurti* (Ojai, CA: Edwin House).

Spodek, Bernard. 1985. "Reflections in Early Childhood Education." *Journal of Curriculum Theorizing* 6 (3): 54–64.

Steiner, George. 1978. *Martin Heidegger.* New York: Viking.

Steiner, Rudolf. 1968. *Essentials of Education.* Hudson, NY: Anthroposophic Press.

Suares, Carlo. 1953. *Krishnamurti and the Unity of Man.* Bombay: Chetana.

Tagore, Rabindranath. 1913. *Gitanjali (Song Offerings).* Preface by W. B. Yeats. London: Macmillan.

Taylor, Frederick Winslow. 1911. *Principles of Scientific Management.* New York: Harper & Brothers.

Thapan, Meenakshi. (1991) 2006. *Life at School: An Ethnographic Study.* Revised ed. Oxford University Press: New Delhi.

Thuruthiyil, Scaria. 1999. *The Joy of Creative Living: Radical Revolution of the Mind. An Approach Proposed by Jiddu Krishnamurti.* Rome: LAS.

Tillich, Paul. 1952. *The Courage to Be.* New Haven: Yale University Press.

Tyler, Ralph. 1949. *Basic Principles of Curriculum and Instruction.* Chicago: University of Chicago Press.

Vas, Luis S. R. 1971. *The Mind of J. Krishnamurti.* Bombay: Jaico Publishing House.

———. 2004. *J Krishnamurti: Great Liberator or Failed Messiah?* New Delhi: Motilal Banarsidas Publishers Private.

Vernon, Roland. 2002. *Star in the East: Krishnamurti—The Invention of a Messiah.* Boulder, CO: Sentient.

Veto, P. 2012. "Tinker, Tailor, Soldier, Sailor, Rich Man, Poor Man, Beggar Man, Thief: Where Is the Teacher? Looking at Our Reflection in the Public Sphere." Master's of Education Capstone Paper, University of British Columbia, Vancouver.

Vyas, Savitri. 1989. *A Critical Study of J. Krishnamurti's Educational Thoughts.* Ahmedabad: Bhagavati.

Whitty, Geoff. 1985. *Sociology and School Knowledge.* London: Metheun.

Wolfson, Bernice J. 1985a. "Closing Remarks." *Journal of Curriculum Theorizing.* 6 (3): 65.

———. 1985b. "Preface: Special Issue in Commemoration of James B. Macdonald, 1925–1983." *Journal of Curriculum Theorizing.* 6 (3): 5–7.

INDEX

Macdonald, Bradley J., 30
Macdonald, James B., xii, xvii–xix, 1,
    3, 5, 16, 19–21, 23–31, 33,
    35–37, 41, 44, 45, 47, 59, 61,
    62, 67, 71–73, 95, 97–110,
    112–117, 119–123, 125,
    127–129, 132, 139, 140, 142,
    143, 152, 157–161
Machine(s), 15, 46, 61, 69, 83, 143
MacMurray, John, 103
Macro-theories, 153
    correspondence, 153
    hegemonic, 153
    reproduction, 153
Madanapalle (India), 20
Mahabharata, 64
Management, 5, 73, 102, 105, 154
    Managerial-disciplinary, 107
    Managerial techniques, 61
Manipulating, 72, 113
Mankind, 1, 41, 48
Mansbridge, Jane, xvii
Manuals, 102
Market, 59, 75, 105, 128
Martin, Donald Wesley, 142
Martin, Raymond, 21, 23, 142
Marx, xvii, 81, 86
    Marxian theory, 44
    Marxism, 34, 40, 56
    Marxist
        conceptualization(s), 15, 44
        disposition, 40
        ideas, 153
        solution, 39
        theory, 15, 46
    Marxist and neo-Marxist
        analyses, 138, 146
        conceptualizations, 81
        education scholars and activists, 34
        theories, 6, 34
Massachusetts Institute of Technology, 87
Master narratives, 5
Materialism, 44, 67, 152
    Materialistic conceptions, 138
    Materialistic education, 22
    Matter, 94, 115

Mathew, Rama, 145
Maximal condition, 98
McLaren, Peter, 6, 138
Measure(s), 2, 44, 46, 79, 105, 121, 150
    achievement, 102
    Measurable, 5, 73, 101, 102
    Measurement, 44, 54, 147
Mechanistic vision of science, 149
Mechanization, 44
Media, 123, 134
Mediocrity, 36, 68, 71, 103
Meditation, xviii, 4, 11, 12, 22, 30, 32,
    55, 80, 84, 86, 87, 90, 91, 105,
    110, 113, 128, 129, 137, 140,
    143, 144, 150, 154–156, 159
Meditative curriculum, 108, 109, 117,
    127, 128, 137, 158
Meditative education, 106, 107, 162
Meditative inquiry (inquiries), xi, xii,
    xvii, xviii, 1, 2, 4, 6, 8–10,
    12–17, 19, 20, 22, 24, 26, 28,
    30, 32, 34, 36–38, 40–42, 44,
    46, 48, 50, 52, 54, 56, 57, 60,
    62, 64, 66, 68, 70, 72, 74,
    76–95, 97–117, 119, 120, 122,
    124–129, 131–135, 137–139,
    148, 154, 156
Meditative practices, dances, and music,
    139
Meditative state, 8, 59, 93, 111, 124
Meditative therapies, 128
Meditative understanding, 57
Memoirs, xviii, 142
Memory (memories), 2, 7, 11, 37, 41,
    43, 51, 52, 56, 57, 64, 78, 79,
    86, 88–90, 92, 93, 124, 139,
    146, 150, 151
Mendizza, Michael, 23, 142
Menon, Shyam, 33, 145
Mental asylums, 121
Method(s), 5, 7, 8, 12, 15, 19, 25, 28,
    84, 87, 88, 95, 104, 105, 109,
    140, 144, 159
Method-centric education, 105
Methods of meditation, 140, 159
Mexico, 145

CPSIA information can be obtained at www.ICGtesting.com
Printed in the USA
LVOW10*1914150514

385950LV00012B/321/P